OECD Skills Studies

Supporting Entrepreneurship and Innovation in Higher Education in Ireland

This work is published under the responsibility of the Secretary-General of the OECD. The opinions expressed and arguments employed herein do not necessarily reflect the official views of the OECD member countries or the European Union.

This document, as well as any data and any map included herein are without prejudice to the status of or sovereignty over any territory, to the delimitation of international frontiers and boundaries and to the name of any territory, city or area.

Please cite this publication as:
OECD/EU (2017), *Supporting Entrepreneurship and Innovation in Higher Education in Ireland*, OECD Skills Studies, OECD Publishing, Paris.
http://dx.doi.org/10.1787/9789264270893-en

ISBN 978-92-64-27088-6 (print)
ISBN 978-92-64-27089-3 (PDF)
ISBN 978-92-64-18843-3 (ePub)

Series: OECD Skills Studies
ISSN 2307-8723 (print)
ISSN 2307-8731 (online)

European Union
Catalogue number: NC-02-17-204-EN-C (print)
Catalogue number: NC-02-17-204-EN-N (PDF)
ISBN 978-92-78-41449-8 (print)
ISBN 978-92-78-41450-4 (PDF)

Photo credits: Original cover illustration by FKT © Anna_leni/Shutterstock for the circle of pictos Square graduation cap : original creation by Freepik

Corrigenda to OECD publications may be found on line at: *www.oecd.org/about/publishing/corrigenda.htm*.
© OECD/EU 2017

You can copy, download or print OECD content for your own use, and you can include excerpts from OECD publications, databases and multimedia products in your own documents, presentations, blogs, websites and teaching materials, provided that suitable acknowledgment of the source and copyright owner is given. All requests for public or commercial use and translation rights should be submitted to *rights@oecd.org*. Requests for permission to photocopy portions of this material for public or commercial use shall be addressed directly to the Copyright Clearance Center (CCC) at *info@copyright.com* or the Centre français d'exploitation du droit de copie (CFC) at *contact@cfcopies.com*.

Preface

Our higher education institutions play a critical role in the development of Ireland's economy and its innovation system. The output and impact of these institutions, both individually and collectively, is central to the achievement of our ambition to sustain national and regional economic growth and build a fair and compassionate society.

Ireland's higher education institutions already perform well across a range of metrics and there has been significant reform across the system in recent years. However, we cannot be complacent. We need to ensure that our institutions become more entrepreneurial and innovative in nature, and that they continually seek to learn both from good practice within the system and internationally. We therefore welcome the publication of this comprehensive review of entrepreneurship and innovation.

The relationship between Ireland and the OECD on education matters has been long and productive. In the area of higher education, an OECD review of our system in the mid 2000s led directly to a major re-configuration of how our higher education system is managed today.

This most recent collaboration through the HEInnovate methodology, a partnership initiative by the European Commission and the OECD, has provided an opportunity to explore a range of issues relevant to supporting entrepreneurship and innovation in higher education. Entrepreneurial skills are a crucial part of the competences that graduates require more and more, in order to be able to compete in an increasingly challenging and globally competitive jobs market. Our institutions are ideally placed to encourage and develop these graduate skills and attributes. We particularly welcome the whole of institution approach adopted in the review and the findings in respect of good practice in our institutions.

There has been significant engagement by Irish higher education institutions both with the HEInnovate self-assessment tool and with the country review process. The review team have consulted widely and have drawn on national and international expertise. As part of their work they met with representatives and stakeholders in individual institutions and with regional and national stakeholders, agencies and departments. We welcome the enthusiasm of so many to engage with this process for improvement.

We commend the work of the Review Team and all those associated with the endeavour and look forward to working with higher education institutions to further develop their capacity and systemise good practice in this important area. We want to ensure that our education system is more responsive to the needs of our economy and society, but importantly, to the needs of the learners.

Mary Mitchell O'Connor TD
Minister of State for Higher Education

John Halligan TD
Minister of State for Training, Skill, Innovation and Research and Development

Preface

Higher education institutions (HEIs) play a critical role in providing the high-level skills the modern economy needs, assisting talented people to transition into employment, generating and disseminating knowledge, driving innovation, and working together with business, government and civil society to promote economic and social development. However, to reach their full potential, HEIs must adapt their organisational approaches, and better integrate research activities, teaching methods and external engagement practices.

Priorities for change include integrating new teaching methods into the curriculum; developing new activities to stimulate entrepreneurial mindsets; providing support to start-ups; strengthening knowledge exchange and collaboration with business and the wider world, and taking a more international approach to HEI activities. Governments can support the evolution of more innovative and entrepreneurial HEIs by adapting the incentives and support structures within their education systems to be more relevant, and through specific public programmes at national and regional levels that support new approaches in HEIs in areas such as teaching and learning, knowledge exchange and start-up support.

Pioneering initiatives are emerging in a number of HEIs. They need to be broader, more systematic and taken forward by HEI leaders in collaboration with key stakeholders. This is the aim of HEInnovate, a joint initiative by the European Commission and the OECD. HEInnovate is a guiding framework that provides inspiration and assistance for governments and HEIs to stimulate innovation and entrepreneurship. It includes an online self-assessment tool (*www.heinnovate.eu*) covering the seven dimensions of the innovative and entrepreneurial HEI. This enables HEIs to organise a participatory stock-taking exercise to review achievements and identify areas for improvement. Available in all EU Member State languages, it includes good practice case studies and workshop materials. Beyond supporting individual HEIs, the European Commission and the OECD implement country reviews in partnership with governments to advance change at higher education system level. Ireland was one of the first countries to participate in the HEInnovate country reviews.

Irish HEIs offer many examples of good practice, based on a strong and growing engagement with industry and local communities. This report provides insights into the approaches taken to establish new learning environments, strong interdisciplinary education and research, and effective knowledge exchange. It also identifies important areas for further improvement at government and HEI level. We believe that this report offers valuable lessons for policy makers, HEI leaders and staff, and other stakeholders in Ireland and beyond.

Mari Kiviniemi
OECD Deputy Secretary-General

Martine Reicherts
Director General for Education, Youth,
Sport and Culture, European Commission

Acknowledgements

The HEInnovate country review of Ireland was a collaborative effort between the Centre for Entrepreneurship, SMEs, Local Development and Tourism of the Organisation for Economic Co-operation and Development (OECD), the Directorate General for Education and Culture of the European Commission, the Department for Education and Skills of Ireland, the Irish Higher Education Authority and Quality and Qualifications Ireland.

A key source of information for this report were study visits to University College of Cork (UCC), Dublin City University (DCU), Dundalk Institute of Technology (DkIT), Galway Mayo Institute of Technology (GMIT), Limerick Institute of Technology (LIT) and University of Limerick (UL). These study visits were organised by the local HEInnovate co-ordinators: Brian O'Flaherty (UCC), Emer Ní Bhrádaigh (DCU), Irene McCausland (DkIT), Des Foley (GMIT), Terry Twomey (LIT), and Christine Brennan (UL). Their enthusiasm, commitment and support were crucial for the review.

Sections of this report were drafted by Richard Thorn, President Emeritus of Sligo Institute of Technology in Ireland (Chapter 1), Ruaidhri Neavyn, Policy Advisor to the Higher Education Authority and President Emeritus of several Institutes of Technology in Ireland (Chapters 1 and 2), Andrea-Rosalinde Hofer, OECD (Chapters 2 and 4), Maria Helena Nazaré, Rector Emeritus of the University of Aveiro, Portugal (Chapter 3), Louise Kempton, Senior Research Associate at the Centre for Urban and Rural Development Studies at Newcastle University, United Kingdom (Chapter 5), Andrew Gibson, Senior Research Assistant at the Higher Education Policy Research Unit (HEPRU) at the Dublin Institute of Technology, Ireland (Chapter 5), and Gabi Kaffka, PhD candidate in Entrepreneurship Studies at Twente University in the Netherlands (Chapter 3). This report was prepared by Andrea-Rosalinde Hofer under the supervision of Jonathan Potter, both of the OECD. Juliette Edwards, Peter Baur and Denis Crowley from the Directorate General for Education and Culture of the European Commission participated in various review activities. Pedro Saraiva from the University of Coimbra in Portugal provided useful comments on the draft report.

This report benefited greatly from knowledge shared by those who participated in the meetings during the study visits. Additional information was collected through a survey of all public Universities and Institutes of Technology in Ireland. Instrumental for the implementation of the review process were Deirdre McDonnell and Joanne Tobin in the Department of Education and Skills, Ruaidhri Neavyn, Richard Thorn and Ellen Hazelkorn in the Higher Education Authority, and Barbara Kelly of Quality and Qualifications Ireland.

The authors are also grateful to Joseph Tixier, Guia Bianchi, Eleanor Davies and Francois Iglesias of the LEED Programme for their invaluable role in providing research and technical assistance, to Kay Olbison for proofreading, and to Janine Treves and Carmen Fernandez Biezma of the OECD Public Affairs and Communications Department.

Table of contents

Abbreviations and acronyms 10
Reader's guide 13
Executive summary 19

Chapter 1. **Overview of the Irish higher education system** 23
    Higher education providers 24
    Student numbers 24
    Resources in Irish higher education 26
    Higher education policy framework 31
    Ireland's national innovation system 37

    Notes 44
    References 44

Chapter 2. **Applying HEInnovate to higher education in Ireland** 47
    Leadership and governance 48
    Organisational capacity: Funding, people and incentives 52
    Entrepreneurial teaching and learning 55
    Preparing and supporting entrepreneurs 60
    Knowledge exchange and collaboration 63
    The internationalised institution 66
    Measuring impact 68
    Recommendations for public policy action 71
    Recommendations for higher education institutions 72

    Notes 73
    References 73

Chapter 3. **Enhancing the organisational capacity of Ireland's higher education institutions** 75
    Introduction 76
    Analysis and findings 78
    Conclusions 86

    Notes 87
    References 87

Chapter 4. **Building entrepreneurial capacity through teaching and learning** 89
    Introduction 90
    Analysis and findings 90
    Conclusions 106

    Notes 106
    References 106

Chapter 5. **Enhancing the impact of Ireland's higher education institutions** 109
    Introduction. 110
    Analysis and findings. 110
    Conclusions 125
    Notes. 126
    References 126

Annex. **HEInnovate framework and good practice statements.** 129

Tables

1.1.	Student numbers in Irish higher education institutions (2014/15).	25
1.2.	Student numbers in Irish higher education institutions by qualifications framework levels (2014/15)	25
1.3.	Distribution of new entrants in Irish higher education institutions across disciplines (2014/15)	25
1.4.	Weighting of subject groups in the core grant allocation to Irish higher education institutions.	27
1.5.	Composition of total recurrent income of Irish higher education institutions, 2007/08 to 2014/15	28
1.6.	Actual and projected expenditure per student in Ireland (2008-15).	29
1.7.	Staffing in Irish public higher education institutions (2011-16)	31
1.8.	Enterprise Ireland support for research and innovation activities in higher education institutions	38
1.9.	Irish Research Council support for industry mobility of early-stage researchers	40
1.10.	Entrepreneurship education activities in the institutional compacts of Irish higher education institutions (2016)	44

Figures

1.1.	Higher education expenditure on R&D in Ireland 2004-10	30
2.1.	Entrepreneurship objectives of Irish higher education institutions.	49
2.2.	Measures to enhance participation in entrepreneurship education	50
2.3.	Strategic local development partners of Irish higher education institutions . .	52
2.4.	Financing entrepreneurship support in Irish higher education institutions . .	53
2.5.	Rewarding excellent performance in Irish higher education institutions.	55
2.6.	Target groups of entrepreneurship education activities in Irish HEIs	56
2.7.	Teaching methods in Irish higher education	57
2.8.	Teaching methods in entrepreneurship courses in Irish higher education . . .	57
2.9.	Advertising extra-curricular entrepreneurship activities in Irish higher education.	58
2.10.	Partners of Irish higher education institutions for entrepreneurship education . . .	59
2.11.	Target groups for entrepreneurship support in Irish higher education institutions	61
2.12.	Offer and demand for start-up support measures	62
2.13.	Start-up training offer in Irish higher education institutions.	63
2.14.	Partners of Irish higher education institutions in knowledge exchange activities	65

2.15. Location of knowledge exchange partners of Irish higher education institutions 66
2.16. Internationalisation activities of Irish higher education institutions 67
2.17. Evaluation practice of knowledge exchange activities in Irish higher education. 70
4.1. Teaching and learning recommendations in the Irish Higher Education Strategy 91
4.2. Organisation of co-operative learning in Irish HEIs 97

Follow OECD Publications on:

 http://twitter.com/OECD_Pubs

 http://www.facebook.com/OECDPublications

 http://www.linkedin.com/groups/OECD-Publications-4645871

 http://www.youtube.com/oecdilibrary

 http://www.oecd.org/oecddirect/

Abbreviations and acronyms

ACE	Centre for Adult Continuing Education
AHSS	Arts, Humanities and Social Sciences
BERD	Business expenditure on research and development
CAO	Central Applications Office
CARL	Community-Academic Research Links
CEEN	Campus Entrepreneurship Enterprise Network
CERN	European Organisation for Nuclear Research
DCU	Dublin City University
DES	Department of Education and Skills
DJEI	Department of Jobs, Enterprise and Innovation
DkIT	Dundalk Institute of Technology
ECTS	European Credit Transfer and Accumulation System
EI	Enterprise Ireland
ENQA	Quality Assurance Agencies in Higher Education
EPSRC	Engineering and Physical Sciences Research Council
EQAR	European Quality Assurance Register for Higher Education
ERC	European Research Council
EU	European Union
EUA	European University Association
GDP	Gross domestic product
GERD	Gross domestic expenditure on research and development
GMIT	Galway Mayo Institute of Technology
GVA	Gross value added
HEA	Higher Education Authority
HEFCE	Higher Education Funding Council for England
HEI	Higher education institution
HERD	Higher Education Expenditure on research and development
IBEC	Irish Business and Employers Confederation
IC4	Irish Centre for Cloud Computing and Commerce
ICT	Information and communications technology
IDA	Ireland's inward investment promotion agency, formerly the Industrial Development Authority
IOT	Institute of Technology
IOTI	Institutes of Technology Ireland
IUA	Irish Universities Association
IRC	Irish Research Council
KTI	Knowledge Transfer Ireland
LIT	Limerick Institute of Technology

MOOCs	Massive online open courses
NGO	Non-governmental organisation
OECD	Organisation for Economic Co-operation and Development
QQI	Quality and Qualifications Ireland
R&D	Research and development
REAP	Roadmap for Employment-Academic Partnership
RGAM	Recurrent Grant Allocation Model
SFI	Science Foundation Ireland
STEM	Science, Technology, Engineering and Mathematics
UCC	University College of Cork
UL	University of Limerick

Reader's guide

The reader's guide provides information on the HEInnovate conceptual framework and online tool. It presents the methodology used in the Irish county review and concludes with a brief overview of the chapters in this report.

The HEInnovate framework

Conceptual framework

Higher education is changing across European Union and OECD countries and there is a growing expectation from policy makers and society that higher education institutions (HEIs) should evolve into a new type of economic actor. Entrepreneurship and innovation in higher education are no longer only associated with business start-ups and technology transfer but are increasingly understood as core elements of a procedural framework for how organisations and individuals behave. For example, in how links between teaching and research are created and nurtured, how societal engagement and knowledge exchange are organised, how resources are built and managed for effective partnerships, and how new entrepreneurs are supported.

Transforming (traditional) HEIs into entrepreneurial and innovative organisations is neither an easy nor a straightforward endeavour. It requires commitment of resources into areas of change and high impact which, in turn, needs to build on a strategic collaboration between policy makers, HEI leaders, staff, students, and partners in the local economy. The aim of HEInnovate is to stimulate and contribute to this strategic collaboration with a guiding framework that describes the innovative and entrepreneurial higher education institution through a set of good practice criteria that has been distilled from an ongoing analysis of current HEI practices across European Union and OECD countries.

HEInnovate was developed collaboratively by the Directorate-General for Education and Culture (DG EAC) of the European Commission and the Centre for Entrepreneurship, SMEs, Local Development and Tourism of the Organisation for Economic Co-operation and Development (OECD). Also contributing was a network of innovation and entrepreneurship professors and experts from across European Union countries. The stimulus for HEInnovate was the University-Business Forum in March 2011, an annual event organised by the European Commission for HEIs and their key strategic partners. Delegates expressed a need for support and guidance in implementing practices that will help them become more innovative and entrepreneurial institutions.

A working definition was agreed which describes the innovative and entrepreneurial HEI as "designed to empower students and staff to demonstrate enterprise, innovation and creativity in teaching, research, and engagement with business and society. Its activities are directed to enhance learning, knowledge production and exchange in a highly complex and changing societal environment; and are dedicated to create public value via processes of open engagement". How this can be translated into daily practice in HEIs is described through 37 statements, which are organised within the following seven dimensions (please refer to the Annex for the full HEInnovate framework and good practice statements):

1. Leadership and Governance
2. Organisational Capacity: Funding, People and Incentives
3. Entrepreneurial Teaching and Learning

4. Preparing and Supporting Entrepreneurs

5. Knowledge Exchange and Collaboration

6. The Internationalised Institution

7. Measuring the Impact

HEInnovate online tool

A freely available online self-assessment tool (*www.heinnovate.eu*) covering the seven dimensions of the "entrepreneurial university" was developed for HEIs to organise a participatory stock-taking exercise to review achievements and identify areas for improvement. It is possible to involve a wide range of stakeholders (leadership, staff, academic and administrative staff, key partner organisations etc.), and to repeat the exercise over time. Users can choose to remain anonymous and data is accessible only to users. The seven dimensions are available in all EU Member State languages.

Explanations of the statements, a growing number of cases studies, multi-media material and workshop facilitation tools, make the online tool inspirational and very user-friendly. Users can work with all dimensions or choose dimensions that are most relevant for their purpose. For example, users could choose to focus on "Organisational Capacity" and "Knowledge Exchange" if the purpose is to (re)organise collaboration with external stakeholders.

An instant reporting function generates a snapshot of the status quo and potential areas of change in the chosen dimensions, comparing the rating of the user/user group to the global/HEI mean. The report points users to guidance material and case study examples with information on concrete actions that HEIs can undertake to enhance their performance in the respective dimension(s). Results are stored and can be compared over time.

There are various examples of how HEIs have been using the HEInnovate online tool. Several HEIs have been using it to organise a creative consultation process around their institutional strategy (e.g. Manchester Metropolitan University in the UK), to design new cross-faculty education programmes (e.g. University of Aveiro in Portugal), for the re-organisation of entrepreneurship support infrastructure (Dundalk Institute of Technology in Ireland), or for the organisation of knowledge exchange activities (e.g. University of Ruse in Bulgaria).

HEInnovate country review methodology

The seven dimensions and good practice statements are also used for HEInnovate policy and system reviews at country level or regional level. The aim of these reviews is to provide a roadmap for strengthening the innovative and entrepreneurial higher education institution. Following an approach that involves a wide range of stakeholders from within the reviewed country (policy makers, HEI leaders, academic and administrative staff members, researchers etc.) and experts and peers from other countries, key areas of strength and areas for improvement are identified and analysed. Recommendations are presented for policy measures that can be implemented by national and sub-national governments, as well as for actions that HEIs can take to act upon opportunities and overcome barriers. The reviews also help to identify and examine examples of good practice from other countries that could provide relevant inspiration.

Recent HEInnovate country reviews have been undertaken in Bulgaria, Ireland, Poland, Hungary, and the Netherlands and further reviews will be undertaken with interested governments.

Method applied in the country-level review of Ireland

The HEInnovate country review of Ireland was undertaken in collaboration with the Department of Education and Skills Ireland, the Higher Education Authority and Quality and Qualifications Ireland. The methodology used in the Irish review was the same as in other HEInnovate reviews and includes the steps described below.

1. Selection of case study HEIs

The selection of HEIs to be covered in the study visits was undertaken collaboratively by the review partners. Several factors were considered during the selection of HEIs, including type of institution and academic focus (e.g. general university, applied sciences university, etc.), size (e.g. number of students) and location (e.g. rural, urban). Applications were sought from HEIs to participate in the review and subsequently the Department of Education and Skills and the OECD jointly selected five higher education institutions for an in-depth study. These were Galway-Mayo Institute of Technology, Limerick Institute of Technology, University of Limerick, University College of Cork, and Dublin City University. Dundalk Institute of Technology was also included following the recommendation of the Institutes of Technology Ireland[1] (IOTI; the representative body for thirteen of Ireland's institutes of technology) to include an HEI with a unique reach into its surrounding economy.

2. Background report and kick-off workshop

A background report was prepared. It contains information on the Irish higher education system, as well as profiles of the HEIs and regions that were included in the study visit. Material from the background report has been integrated into this report.

A kick-off workshop for the project was held in Dublin in April 2015. Representatives of the HEIs selected for the study visits, the Department for Education and Skills of Ireland, the Higher Education Authority, Quality and Qualifications Ireland and the Department of Jobs, Enterprise and Innovation and Enterprise Ireland participated in the workshop.

The purpose was to familiarise the participants with the HEInnovate tool, the review method, and to identify the following HEInnovate dimensions to be examined in more depth as focus areas of the review. Three dimensions were selected: Organisational Capacity, Entrepreneurial Teaching and Learning, and Measuring Impact. A representative of the OECD Secretariat presented the HEInnovate country-level review methodology and outlined the expectations for participating HEIs. The European Commission presented the HEInnovate tool and explained how the HEIs could use it and benefit from it.

3. Study visits

In October and November 2015, an international review team completed two country visits to Ireland with one-day study visits to the above mentioned six case study HEIs to meet with presidents/rectors and/or vice-presidents/vice-rectors, deans, professors, career offices, technology transfer offices, business incubators, student associations, student and staff start-up companies, students taking entrepreneurship courses, and alumni. In addition to meeting with local and regional representatives, several meetings were held with national stakeholders, including Enterprise Ireland (EI), IDA Ireland, Science Foundation Ireland (SFI), the Irish Research Council (IRC), Quality and Qualifications Ireland (QQI), the Higher Education Authority (HEA), SOLAS (the further education and training authority), the

Department for Education and Skills, the Department of Jobs, Enterprise and Innovation, the Department of Social Protection, and various business representative organisations.

4. HEI Leader Survey

An online survey of HEI leaders was used to complement the information obtained in the background report and the study visits. The questionnaire is based on the HEInnovate framework and contains seven sections. It asks about current and planned practices in i) the strategic directions of the HEI, ii) management of human and financial resources, iii) the teaching and learning environment, iv) knowledge exchange activities, v) internationalisation, vi) entrepreneurship education, and vii) business start-up support. The survey was sent to the Presidents' offices of the seven universities and the 14 institutes of technology. In total, 17 HEIs, including all universities and 10 institutes of technology completed the questionnaire with an overall response rate of 81%. The survey response rates per HEI type are as follows: universities (100%), institutes of technology (71%).

5. Report and workshop

This report was prepared with inputs from the international review team and the local review co-ordinator, drawing on information gathered during the study visits and from the two online surveys. An interim report summarising key findings and preliminary recommendations was circulated in December 2015 for comments to the Department for Education and Skills. Written feedback on observations from the study visits and suggested actions were sent to the case study HEIs.

A draft report was presented and discussed in an interactive workshop hosted by the Dublin City University in May 2016. Following the workshop, the OECD Secretariat finalised the report, taking into account written feedback and contributions made in the workshop.

The content of this report

Chapter 1 presents the Irish higher education system. It describes the multi-step ladder system of qualifications that allows students to step in and out of undergraduate education. It presents trends in student numbers and resources of higher education institutions. Further it provides an overview of recent policy initiatives, such the National Strategy for Higher Education to 2030, the introduction of the System Performance Framework and the establishment of the Regional Skills Fora and the Regional Cluster initiative.

Chapter 2 presents key review findings and recommendations. The analysis is aligned to the HEInnovate framework with its seven dimensions and 37 statements. It covers a holistic approach to supporting entrepreneurship and innovation, including strategy, governance and resources, practices in organising education, research and engagement with business and society, and measuring impact.

Chapters 3, 4 and 5 expand on the key findings and recommendations presented in Chapter 2. Chapter 3 examines organisational capacity from a system-level perspective and discusses the current restructuring of the higher education system, the steering mechanisms and funding of research in higher education institutions. The chapter discusses regional collaborative initiatives involving HEIs and provides suggestions for their further development. The chapter also reviews current practices undertaken by higher education institutions to enhance and sustain their organisational capacity primarily with regard to research and knowledge exchange.

Chapter 4 focuses on teaching and learning in Irish HEIs. It starts with an overview of the national level approaches in this regard, namely the teaching and learning recommendations in the National Strategy for Higher Education to 2030 and the establishment of the National Forum for the Enhancement of Teaching and Learning in Higher Education. The chapter analyses various approaches to enhance the capacity of students for entrepreneurship and reviews the role of higher education institutions in lifelong learning. The chapter also discusses the role of education in translating scientific research into societal relevance and presents good practice examples of how to incentivise student participation in knowledge exchange activities.

Chapter 5 reviews the impact of higher education and the possible results of a greater emphasis on entrepreneurship and innovation. There are significant opportunities to impact the local economy, not only directly but in a wide range of indirect ways, both on the supply and demand side. However, as discussed in the chapter, there is also a range of tensions that need to be understood and carefully managed by the HEIs themselves, their local partners and national policy makers if impacts are to be effectively delivered.

Note

1. Since this country review was undertaken, a new representative body for institutes of technology has been established called the Technological Higher Education Association (THEA). THEA is the representative body for all fourteen institutes of technology.

Executive summary

Study context

Higher education is changing across the European Union and OECD countries. Entrepreneurship and innovation in higher education are no longer only associated with business start-ups and technology transfer but are increasingly understood as core elements of a procedural framework for how organisations and individuals behave. For example, in how they create and nurture links between teaching and research, how they organise engagement and knowledge exchange, how they manage effective partnerships with a range of stakeholders, and how they support nascent entrepreneurs. Transforming (traditional) higher education institutions (HEIs) into entrepreneurial and innovative organisations is neither an easy nor a straightforward endeavour. Major obstacles may lie deep in the higher education system, for example if knowledge exchange and engagement with business and society are not included in the HEI's core functions or core funding.

A strong and growing engagement agenda with industry and local communities, the emergence of new learning environments and interdisciplinary research teams make Ireland an ideal country to take a closer look into the ongoing transformation processes in HEIs. This report presents evidence-based analysis of the current strategies and practices to support innovation and entrepreneurship in higher education, using the HEInnovate guiding framework, jointly developed by the European Commission and the OECD.

Key findings

Irish higher education plays a fundamental role in fostering entrepreneurial career paths for students and graduates. The wide and rich range of initiatives includes undergraduate and postgraduate courses, work-based learning, business start-up and incubation programmes, mentoring and coaching to mention but a few. President's Awards and national competitions, such as the all-Ireland business plan competition, are also important to showcase achievements by staff and students in HEIs.

Several of the HEIs visited for this review demonstrated that innovation and entrepreneurship are embedded within their strategy and in the organisation as a whole. This provides fertile grounds, not only for learner development and a wide application of research results through business and in society, but also for the definition of new interdisciplinary approaches in education and research. The activities are supported and driven by senior management, usually by a combination of the Vice-president for research and the heads of faculty. A strong emphasis is placed on staff development programmes.

HEIs in Ireland play multiple roles in their local environments and are, particularly outside the capital city, pivotal drivers of economic, social and community development. Their success in attracting third-party funding shows their importance as catalysts in unlocking collaborative research which smaller organisations, especially small and medium-sized enterprises, may not have the capacity or networks to pursue alone. The involvement of the Arts, Humanities and Social Sciences (AHSS) in this appears to be somewhat less developed than Science, Technology, Engineering and Mathematics (STEM). Still, there are several examples of good practice which should be replicated in all faculties.

The sustainability of these multiple roles of HEIs is a question of institutional autonomy and organisational capacity, of which the amount, allocation and duration of funding are key determining factors. For their entrepreneurial and innovation activities, including entrepreneurship education and start-up support initiatives, the HEIs are heavily and in some cases almost totally dependent upon temporary project funding. This position has become even more pronounced during the recent economic crisis, which has seen a significant reduction in state funding for the higher education system. This is impacting on the range and sustainability of activities, as the HEIs have had to be fluid and flexible in their financial strategies and focused on maintaining core activities principally in the teaching and learning arena.

The higher education system is currently structured in the form of a mission-diverse and complementary system with highly collaborative HEIs, in which diversity, high quality and performance can be maintained and strengthened. National initiatives to support the further development of the higher education system include the introduction of a new system performance framework, strategic dialogue and institutional compacts and the establishment of Regional Skills Fora and Regional Clusters.

Effective internationalisation strategies have evolved from the active participation of HEIs in international networks. A new sector-wide strategy was recently published and discussions are underway regarding the extension of the "stay back" period to two years for cohorts of international graduates with relevant in-demand skills.

There are many examples of innovative and impactful activities taking place in HEIs. However it might be fair to say that individual HEIs, research groups and the sector as a whole have not been effective at telling their story and making the case for further funding and investment. While there are numerous sources of information on various activities, these are not being translated effectively enough into details of their actual impacts in terms of the economy and society as a whole. It will also be important to enhance inter- and transdisciplinary research initiatives and their impact.

The higher education sector needs to speak with one voice in describing and aggregating the impact of its core functions in education, research and engagement in order to win the support of policy makers and the public for continued and additional investment. There are already examples of good practice present in the Irish HEIs. Information about these needs to be made widely available and such good practice should be replicated and promoted.

Key recommendations

For public policy action

- Enhance collaboration between policy structures and state agencies involved in supporting entrepreneurship and innovation in HEIs.
- Broaden the scope for multi- and transdisciplinary research initiatives in research priorities, and in the effort to mobilise HEIs in local, regional and national development.

- Review current employment control restrictions in higher education to allow for enhanced engagement activities with business and society.
- Continue targeted state investment in internationalisation initiatives.
- Support HEIs in creating collaborative and mentor links with innovative and entrepreneurial HEIs abroad.
- Introduce a system-wide exercise to document and assess the impact of entrepreneurship and innovation in higher education.

For higher education institutions
- Expand entrepreneurship education across all disciplines and increase the number of interdisciplinary education activities.
- Increase the number of places available on venture creation programmes, particularly for students and alumni.
- Incentivise and support staff engagement in knowledge exchange activities.
- Enhance collaboration with small and medium-sized enterprises through a single "front door" approach.

Chapter 1

Overview of the Irish higher education system

This chapter presents the Irish higher education system. It describes the multi-step ladder system of qualifications that allows students to step in and out of undergraduate education. It presents trends in student numbers and resources of higher education institutions. Further it provides an overview of recent policy initiatives, such as the National Strategy for Higher Education to 2030, the System Performance Framework and the Strategic Dialogue and institutional performance compacts with individual higher education institutions, and the establishment of the Regional Clusters of higher education institutions. These will be further discussed in subsequent chapters.

Higher education providers

Higher education in Ireland is provided by public and private higher education institutions (HEIs). The public HEIs include seven universities, fourteen institutes of technology (IOTs) and seven colleges of education, several of which are in the process of merging with universities, and five colleges recognised by the National University of Ireland. In addition, a number of other third-level institutions provide specialist education in such fields as art and design, medicine, business studies, rural development, theology, music and law. Universities operate under the 1997 Universities Act, which sets out the objects and functions of a university, the structure and role of governing bodies, staffing arrangements, composition and role of academic councils and sections relating to property, finance and reporting. The governing authorities are required to see that strategic development plans are in place, along with procedures for evaluating teaching and research. The legislative framework preserves the academic freedom of the universities and respects the diverse traditions and institutional autonomy of each university. Institutes of Technology operate primarily under the 1992 Regional Technical Colleges Act and the 2006 Institutes of Technology Act. The latter provided IOTs with a similar relationship to the Higher Education Authority (HEA) as the universities. It also provided IOTs with greater autonomy, improved governance and a statutory guarantee of academic freedom. Colleges operate under various pieces of legislation. Most public HEIs are under the purview of the HEA but a small number are directly funded by the Department of Education and Skills (DES). Further, several private colleges receive state funding from competitive programmes such as through the recent labour market activation initiative called Springboard.

Approximately 90% of higher education students in Ireland attend public institutions. Private higher education providers do not generally provide information on registered students to the HEA. A study undertaken for the HEA in 2012, estimated that the private colleges account for approximately 10% of the total higher education student population in Ireland (DES, 2015). The private HEIs are mostly located in Dublin and have significant presence in part time, international education and in labour market activation programmes in the Dublin area.[1]

Student numbers

The higher education component of Ireland's qualifications framework comprises: Level 6 (Higher Certificate), Level 7 (Ordinary Bachelor Degree), Level 8 (Honours Bachelor Degree/Higher Diploma), Level 9 (Masters Degree), and Level 10 (Doctorate). The majority of students are enrolled on Level 8 degree programmes. Between 2011 and 2014 there was a 7.1% increase in the number of graduates.

Applications for entry to undergraduate courses in universities, IOTs and colleges are processed by the Central Applications Office (CAO). The aim of the system is to process applications centrally and to deal with them in an efficient and fair manner. The participating HEIs retain the function of making decisions relating to admissions. In 2014/15 there were 217 520 students enrolled in HEA-designated HEIs, including full-time, part-time and remote students, and of these 42 464 were new undergraduate entrants, that is a 17% increase in the seven years from 2007/08. Table 1.1 provides a breakdown across the three major sectors, and Table 1.2 shows the distribution across the different levels of the qualifications framework.

Table 1.1. **Student numbers in Irish higher education institutions (2014/15)**

Sector	Number	Percentage
Universities	113 703	52%
Institutes of Technology	91 013	42%
Colleges	12 804	6%
Total	217 520	100%

Source: Higher Education Authority Ireland (2017a), Student enrolment numbers, www.hea.ie/node/1557 (accessed 11 February 2017).

Table 1.2. **Student numbers in Irish higher education institutions by qualifications framework levels (2014/15)**

Sector	Number	Percentage
Level 6 (Higher Certificate)	12 679	6%
Level 7 (Ordinary Bachelor Degree)	25 493	12%
Level 8 (Honours Bachelor Degree/Higher Diploma)	125 612	58%
Levels 9 and 10		
taught postgraduate	29 551	14%
research postgraduate	9 606	4%

Source: Higher Education Authority Ireland (2017a), Student enrolment numbers, www.hea.ie/node/1557 (accessed 11 February 2017).

In 2014/2015, the number of international students in Ireland studying in a full-time course for a semester or more in a public or private HEI was 33 118, of whom 11 678 are EU students and 21 440 are non-EU. This represents an increase of 58% in the number of international students since 2010/11.

According to most recent data the highest number of new entrants in universities is in humanities and arts (28%), followed by both social science, business and law, which has the highest number of new entrants in institutes of technology and the second highest in universities (24%). The lowest number of entrants in both is recorded for agriculture and veterinary science. Table 1.3 shows the percentage distribution of new entrants across different disciplines in both universities and IOTs in 2014/15.

Table 1.3. **Distribution of new entrants in Irish higher education institutions across disciplines (2014/15)**

Discipline	Percentage	
	Institutes of Technology	Universities
Education	–	2%
Humanities and Arts	11%	28%
Social Science, Business and Law	24%	24%
Science	18%	19%
Engineering, Manufacturing and Construction	16%	7%
Agriculture and Veterinary Science	2%	2%
Health and Welfare	14%	15%
Combined	–	2%
Services	14%	–

Source: Higher Education Authority Ireland (2017a), Student enrolment numbers, www.hea.ie/node/1557 (accessed 11 February 2017).

A multi-step ladder system of qualifications

At undergraduate level, Ireland has introduced a multi-step ladder system of qualifications. This allows students to step in and out of undergraduate education. This system has several advantages. It helps to improve retention and progression rates within the higher education system by allowing students to obtain a full qualification at an earlier stage within the undergraduate cycle. Students can decide on how to progress with their undergraduate studies in terms of the level at which they enter and exit. The flexibility to enter and exit at different levels means that students can gain exposure to industry and business, both at home and abroad, and return to their studies at a later stage.

Resources in Irish higher education

Current funding model

The current funding model of higher education is kept under ongoing review with the primary objective of ensuring that it appropriately supports the national objectives set for the higher education system. The introduction of performance funding and the provision of incentivisation funding for clusters of collaborating institutions represents a major new departure. Funding discussions between the HEA and the HEIs are now integrated into the strategic dialogue process (see below) rather than standalone budget meetings as was previously the case.

The recently published Report of the Expert Group on Future Funding (Cassell's Report) states that Ireland's higher education system needs a substantial increase in the level of investment to ensure that the system is able to deliver fully on its role in supporting national economic and social development. The report also states that the investment must be linked to enhanced quality and verification of outcomes. The report points to a number of different potential ways to provide additional funding for higher education, including increased state funding, increased state funding with a student loan system and an increased contribution from enterprise (HEA, 2016a).

Under current funding arrangements, the HEA allocates exchequer funding to HEIs through the Recurrent Grant Allocation Model (RGAM) which was initially introduced for the universities in 2006 and for the IOTs from 2011, and has three main elements:

- An annual recurrent "block" grant that is allocated to each institution based on known formulae relating to the number of students and their subject areas. The principle behind the grant is that it should be fair, simple, transparent, that there should be uniformity in the core grant allocation for students in the same broad areas (regardless of the institution at which they study), and that there should be recognition of the extra costs that arise for students from under-represented backgrounds and research students.

- Performance related funding that is allocated to institutions based on benchmarked performance in delivering on national objectives set for their sector. This type of funding is being phased in (from 2014), and it is expected to account for up to 10% of annual funding in time.

- Targeted/strategic funding that supports national strategic priorities and which may be allocated to the HEIs on a competitive basis.

The annual grant that HEIs receive is allocated as a block grant, and how funds are allocated internally (for example, across faculties and between research and teaching) is a matter for each institution. There are two main elements to the allocation model, a core grant and a grant in lieu of undergraduate fees. As an incentive to maximise the other income that HEIs may earn, such income is not taken into account in the grant allocation.

The RGAM includes a moderating mechanism that ensures that the grant allocation per HEI may not change by more than 2% (increase or decrease) from year to year. The purpose of this is to prevent large swings in allocations and to help institutions maintain financial stability.

The core grant is allocated based on a standard per capita amount for each student, "weighted" by the relative cost of the student's subject group. This system of weighting draws significantly from that used by the Higher Education Funding Council for England (HEFCE) and reflects the fact that broad groups of subjects have different levels of resource requirements. The student numbers used for calculating the amount are those as at 1 March in the previous academic year. Table 1.4 shows the four subject groups and their weighting.

Table 1.4. **Weighting of subject groups in the core grant allocation to Irish higher education institutions**

Subject price group	Subject price group weighting
A. Clinical stages of undergraduate Medicine (transitional weighting)	2.3
A. Undergraduate Dentistry, Veterinary	4.0
B. Laboratory-based subjects (Science, Engineering, pre-clinical Medicine and Dentistry)	1.7
C. Subjects with a studio, laboratory or fieldwork element	1.3
D. All other subjects	1.0

Source: DES (2015).

An adjustment is made within the core grant allocation to reflect the costs to the institutions of attracting and supporting students who come from non-traditional backgrounds. An additional weighting of 33% is currently used. The current funding model also includes an adjustment to equalise overall funding provided for level 6, 7 and 8 programmes in the IOTs, thereby removing the previous financial disincentive in relation to the provision of level 6 and 7 programmes. Most recently, a specific detailed report on funding in the IOTs (HEA, 2016b) has recommended an adjustment be applied to STEM funding for IOTs in recognition of the declining impact of STEM weightings as a consequence of increasing student contribution and decreasing RGAM allocations.

Allocation of funding based on research is organised in the following way. In addition to weighting research students, 5% of the core allocation is top-sliced (exclusive of the grant in lieu of tuition fees) and allocated on the basis of research criteria (research degrees awarded and contract research income per academic staff). This element of the model currently applies only to universities.

Funding levels and trends

Between 2008 and 2014 the total income (from all sources) per student decreased by 22%. The overall level of state funding of HEIs has been declining since 2007/08, and by 2015/16 it was at 51% of total funding, compared to 76% in 2007/08. This continuing decline is in line with public policy measures in relation to increases in the student contribution (student charge or fee) and reductions in overall funding, including income from the student contribution. When taking into account the fact that approximately half of the student charge income is paid indirectly by the Exchequer through student higher education grants, the decline in funding is from 78% of the total in 2008 to 68% in 2013 and to 64% in 2016. This compares with the OECD average of 68% and the EU21 average of 76.4% for 2010, the latest year for which data is available.

By 2016, privately paid student contributions, that is, excluding higher education grants and as distinct from the total of income from non-state sources, have amounted to 19% of total HEI income. Income from research grants and contracts as a proportion of the total income of universities and institutes of technology has increased from EUR 373 million or 13% of income in 2002 to EUR 453 million or 19% of total income in 2011. Table 1.5 shows the changes in the composition of total recurrent income of HEIs from 2007/08 to 2014/15.

Table 1.5. **Composition of total recurrent income of Irish higher education institutions, 2007/08 to 2014/15**

Year	State grant and free fees (EUR million)	Income from student contribution (EUR million)	Other fees and other income (EUR million)	Total recurrent income excluding research (EUR million)	State grant and free fees as a % of total
2007/08	1 397	91	362	1 850	76%
2008/09	1 318	104	407	1 829	72%
2009/10	1 249	187	402	1 838	68%
2010/11	1 179	195	397	1 771	67%
2011/12	1 119	264	400	1 783	63%
2012/13	1 012	302	403	1 717	59%
2013/14	939	338	406	1 683	56%
2014/15	895	382	409	1 686	53%
2015/16	860	427	413	1 700	51%

Notes: This table excludes Royal College of Surgeons of Ireland and international students. It takes account of increased income from student contributions and a further 1% overall net reduction in grants. State grant funding excludes funding in respect of pension costs.
Source: Higher Education Authority (2014a).

Expenditure per student by HEIs (excluding research expenditure) has declined by 15% in the five years to 2013, and the bulk of this decline is accounted for by the growth in student numbers. Expenditure per student will have declined by 24% over the eight years from 2008 to the end of the Strategic Dialogue period in 2016. The HEA considers that the rapid decline in funding per student constitutes a strong warning that it may not be possible to achieve all of the projected future increases in enrolment or that future increases may be delivered at the expense of quality. Table 1.6 presents the actual and projected expenditure per student.

Research funding

Research funding in higher education has decreased in recent years and the vast majority of the research and development (R&D) component of the block grant allocated to cover core teaching and research activities within institutions is spent on salaries and overheads. Ireland does not have a system for allocating core funds to HEIs for research purposes. The core funding is allocated as a block grant, using a formula which top-slices a research element. It is up to the HEIs to determine its internal allocation. As a result of the reductions in the block grant and a period of no capital investments, the research infrastructure in terms of equipment and facilities that were invested during less constrained times are becoming obsolete. To counter this, Science Foundation Ireland has provided funding to HEIs through its Research Infrastructure Programme and there are commitments

Table 1.6. **Actual and projected expenditure per student in Ireland (2008-15)**

Year	Recurrent income/ expenditure (EUR million)	Students (fulltime)	Expenditure per student (EUR)	Percentage change in expenditure per student from 2007/08
2007/08	1 850	157 012	11 783	–
2008/09	1 829	163 149	11 211	-5%
2009/10	1 838	172 917	10 629	-10%
2010/11	1 771	176 780	10 018	-15%
2011/12	1 783	178 522	9 988	-15%
2012/13	1 717	180 461	9 515	-19%
2013/14	1 683	181 694	9 263	-21%
2014/15	1 686	185 226	9 102	-23%
2015/16	1 700	188 943	8 997	-24%

Source: Higher Education Authority (2014a).

to fund capital equipment and to increase human capital as part of Innovation 2020, Ireland's new strategy for research and development, science and technology.

There are three main competitive research funding agencies: the Irish Research Council (IRC), the Health Research Board (HRB) and Science Foundation Ireland (SFI), each with distinct and complementary missions. Other state and semi-state bodies that fund research do so as part of their function (e.g. Teagasc). SFI funds research centres and large projects with economic impact as a priority. The IRC funds smaller, individually focused programmes targeted at human capital development in the research arena. The HRB focuses on the clinical domain and the health system. In addition, Enterprise Ireland focuses on innovation, near market and enterprise competitive supports. Each of these funding sources have their own, often complex processes for responding to calls for applications. There is no common research classification system, which makes sharing data between agencies difficult. Lead times from application to award can be lengthy. Research programmes are all allocated competitively and this means that the HEIs and individual researchers must compete with each other, as well as with other public and private research organisations, both nationally and (in the case of EU funds) internationally.

It is worth noting HEI success in competing for EU research funding. Of the EUR 625 million drawdown under DFP7, the Higher Education Institutions accounted for 65% of total drawdown (EUR 409 million), with Ireland's companies accounting for 26% (EUR 164 million) of total funding secured. More recently, in the period from commencement of Horizon 2020 in January 2014 to September 2016 (latest report available) there were 5 298 applicants from Irish-based organisations in Horizon 2020 proposals. From these, 811 applicants were successful, giving an overall Irish success rate of 15.31% (EU Member State average: 14.13%). Ireland's drawdown in Horizon 2020 in this period was EUR 336 million. The HEIs were the primary beneficiaries, accounting for 59% of all funding. Funding to Private Industry was 31%, with public bodies, research organisations and others (e.g. hospitals) making up the rest (9.9%).

The Innovation 2020 strategy recognises the importance of continuing to support excellent research across all disciplines. The national research prioritisation exercise in 2011/12 identified 14 priority areas where future competitively awarded research funding should be focused. The criteria used to select the areas were:

- The priority area is associated with a large global market or markets in which Irish-based enterprises already compete or can realistically compete.

- Publicly performed R&D in Ireland is required to exploit the priority area and will complement private sector research and innovation in Ireland.
- Ireland has built or is building (objectively measured) strengths in research disciplines relevant to the priority area.
- The priority area represents an appropriate approach to a recognised national challenge and/or a global challenge to which Ireland should respond.

The prioritisation exercise did not affect the balance of funding between the Science, Technology, Engineering and Mathematics (STEM), and Arts Humanities and Social Sciences (AHSS).

Figure 1.1. **Higher education expenditure on R&D in Ireland 2004-10**
Current prices, EUR millions

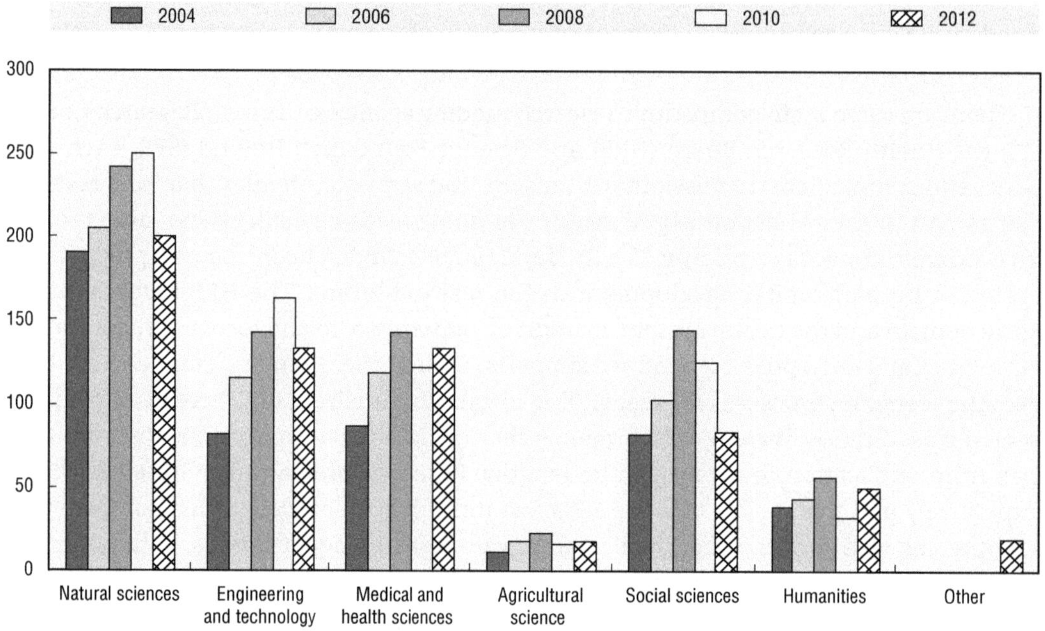

Source: DJEI (2013).

Looking at funding between 2008 and 2012, there has been a reduction in funding for AHSS. In 2008, funding was EUR 201 million and this dropped by 32% or EUR 65 million in 2012 to EUR 134 million. Most of this reduction was in the social sciences area. Other disciplines also saw reductions between 2008 and 2012, but not as much.

In 2013 the Independent Review of Research Prioritisation pointed out that for many research areas, including most of the Humanities and Social Sciences, and basic and applied STEM outside the 14 priority areas, the only national funding schemes available were those administered by the Irish Research Council. These account for 4% of total public investment in R&D and concentrate on individual awards for PhD students and postdoctoral researchers. The report goes on to state that the scarcity of national funding for areas outside the Research Prioritisation, even in some areas where Ireland had significant capacity prior to the Research Prioritisation, may undermine Ireland's ability to respond to emerging or unforeseen areas of opportunity in the future. There is a concern that researchers from those areas will exit the system, with adverse consequences for higher education, skills supply and the broader ecosystem.

Staffing arrangements

The HEIs have absorbed substantial cuts in public funding while meeting demands for increased intake of students and maintaining quality. In this environment of constrained resources, workload management models can support a more sustainable use of resources and greater and more transparent efficiency. It remains particularly difficult, however, to make workload comparisons across disciplines and institutions. As a result of this, most institutional models require further development – mainly in the area of better workload data collection and analysis.

Institutional workload management models have been developed and implemented since 2010 as part of wide-scale reforms of the public sector. A review of staffing arrangements carried out in 2014 found that all universities and most other HEIs have introduced workload management practices since 2010, see Table 1.7 for data relating to staffing (HEA, 2014b).

Table 1.7. **Staffing in Irish public higher education institutions (2011-16)**

Staff numbers	2011	2012	2013	2014	2016
Core staff	17 699	17 280	17 194	17 059	18 022
Core academic staff	9 272	9 041	9 053	9 040	9 475
Core support staff	8 427	8 238	8 141	8 018	8 545
Contract research and specialist staff	4 988	5 308	5 447	6 027	5 849
Contract/specialist academic staff	3 065	3 408	3 253	3 717	3 778
Contract/specialist support staff	1 923	1 900	2 194	2 310	2 071
Total staff	**22 686**	**22 588**	**22 641**	**23 085**	**23 870**
Academic staff	12 336	12 449	12 306	12 757	13 253
Support staff	10 350	10 139	10 335	10 328	10 616

Notes: Numbers given are full-time equivalents.
Source: Higher Education Authority (2014b).

Higher education policy framework

Key actors

The Department of Education and Skills (DES) is the government department responsible for all aspects of education and training in the country. Public policy in higher education and research is informed by the work of the Higher Education Authority (HEA), a statutory state agency established with its own board under the aegis of the DES. The HEA is accountable to the Minister for Education and Skills for the achievement of national outcomes for the higher education sector. It exercises a central oversight role in the higher education system and is the lead agency in the ongoing development of a co-ordinated system of HEIs that have diverse but clear roles appropriate to their individual strengths and are responsive to national strategic objectives. Its responsibilities include i) leading the strategic development of Irish higher education and research; ii) advising the Minister and the Department of Education on all matters relating to higher education; iii) acting as the funding authority for the universities, institutes of technology and other designated HEIs; iv) ensuring effective governance and regulation of HEIs and of the higher education system as a whole; v) promoting equity of access to higher education; and vi) enhancing HEIs' responsiveness to the needs of wider society. A central mission of the HEA is therefore to ensure that higher education and research remain responsive to the social, cultural and economic development of Ireland and its people and support the achievement of national objectives. This includes ensuring that institutional strategies are aligned with national objectives, that there is effective performance management at institutional and system-level, and that due regard is given to institutional autonomy and academic freedom.

The Department of Jobs, Enterprise and Innovation (DJEI) is responsible for developing, promoting and co-ordinating science, technology and innovation policy in Ireland, including opening access to opportunities for Ireland's research and enterprise communities. DJEI is also responsible for Science Foundation Ireland (SFI), which funds oriented basic research and applied research in the areas of Science, Technology, Engineering and Mathematics (STEM), and more recently has seen an expansion of its mandate to cover applied research, as well as for the "Programme for Research in Third Level Institutions", which supports research in humanities, science, technology and the social sciences, including business and law. DJEI also has responsibility for Enterprise Ireland, the agency charged with the development of indigenous enterprise and IDA Ireland, the agency charged with responsibility for foreign direct investments.

Over the past 20 years Ireland has operated on the basis of an emerging European model that places a strong emphasis on institutional autonomy in higher education, and within which HEIs take primary responsibility for quality assurance. An external agency, Quality and Qualifications Ireland (QQI) was established in 2012 as a result of the amalgamation of three existing quality assurance agencies. QQI is responsible for ensuring the effectiveness of the HEIs' internal quality assurance arrangements through external monitoring and review. Public HEIs are self-validating but QQI is responsible for validating programmes in private HEIs and in further education and training providers. The method used in higher education is quite intensive with a separate independent 4-5 person panel visiting the institution/provider for each new programme approval.

Recent policy developments

The National Strategy for Higher Education to 2030

The National Strategy for Higher Education to 2030 was published by the Department of Education and Skills in January 2011 and provides a clear policy framework and context for higher education in Ireland (DES, 2011). The strategy sets out a new vision in which higher education will play a central role in making the country recognised for innovation, competitive enterprise and continuing academic excellence, and an attractive place to live and work.

The strategy re-affirmed the fundamental importance of excellent teaching and learning, quality in research and knowledge transfer, and effective engagement between higher education and society. In particular, it identified the challenge and opportunities that come with growing demand for higher education arising from Ireland's demographic growth, which is relatively unique in the European context. It also recognised the need for the higher education system to be internationally networked and to perform to international benchmarks, and its role in upskilling the workforce.

The strategy made 26 recommendations, the implementation of which is in progress and is having profound effects on higher education in Ireland. The recommendations cover areas as diverse as access, knowledge transfer, institutional consolidation, the development of a sustainable funding base, institutional collaboration through regional and thematic clusters, and performance funding. The most radical recommendation, however, was that instead of considering higher education in Ireland as comprising a set of discrete institutions it should be regarded as a system that as a collective delivered higher education outputs for the country. Underpinning all the recommendations is the idea that higher education in Ireland is best understood as a collective system that delivers the higher education that Ireland needs and within which each individual institution makes its contribution in a way that is consonant with its mission (HEA, 2012). The recommendations ranged across a number of areas, but those that relate to research and engagement with wider society are of most relevance to this review.

In relation to research, the strategy recommends affording a wider focus to the researcher's role, one that might allow for greater mobility of staff between higher education and enterprise, and increase researchers' career opportunities. More specifically, it recommends "mobility of staff … between higher education … and enterprise and the public service … to promote knowledge flows and to capitalise on the expertise within higher education for the benefit of society and the economy". Various mechanisms such as secondments and consultancy are suggested as being mutually beneficial to academics, their institutions, and to wider society.

The strategy also notes that in order to facilitate such collaboration and engagement between higher education and enterprise, review mechanisms and metrics are required to achieve parity of esteem across disciplines, types of research and innovation activities (including knowledge transfer and commercialisation). It also recommends embedding knowledge transfer within HEIs' activities, which should be rewarded accordingly. In this regard, the establishment of Knowledge Transfer Ireland in 2014 (see below) is also relevant DJEI (2016).

As part of the efforts to encourage a broadening of individual researchers' roles, the Strategy calls for HEIs to be more engaged with the wider community, and for this engagement to be embedded in their missions. The specific actions that HEIs need to take to achieve this goal are:

- Encourage greater inward and outward mobility of staff between HEIs, business, industry, and the wider community.
- Respond positively to the continuing professional development needs of the wider community to develop and deliver appropriate modules and programmes in a flexible and responsive way.
- Recognise civic engagement of their students through programme accreditation as is appropriate.
- Put in place procedures and structures that welcome and encourage the involvement of the wider community in a range of activities, including programme design and revision.

As part of these actions, the Strategy calls for the HEA to carry out a national survey of employers as part of the assessment of quality outcomes for the system. Also proposed was a coherent framework of system-wide collaboration between HEIs in so-called Regional Clusters, with a view to improving responsiveness to local and regional economic needs.

The System Performance Framework; Strategic Dialogue and institutional performance compacts

The System Performance Framework includes a set of high-level system indicators relating to the following key system objectives for 2014-16:

1. Meet Ireland's human capital needs across the spectrum of skills through engaged institutions, a diverse mix of provision across the system and through both core funding and specifically targeted initiatives.

2. Promote access for disadvantaged groups and put in place coherent pathways from second-level education, from further education and other non-traditional entry routes.
3. Promote excellence in teaching and learning and assessment to underpin a high quality student experience.
4. Maintain an open and excellent public research system focused on the national priority areas and the achievement of other societal objectives and to maximise research collaborations and knowledge exchange between and amongst public and private sector research actors.
5. Ensure that Ireland's HEIs will be globally competitive and internationally oriented, and Ireland will be a world-class centre of international education.
6. Reform practices and restructure the system for quality and diversity.
7. Increase accountability of autonomous institutions for public funding and against national priorities.

The rollout of the Strategic Dialogue process and the agreement of the institutional performance compacts between the HEA and each HEI is an integral element of the implementation of the System Performance Framework for Higher Education 2014-16, which sets out to align the missions, strategies and profiles of individual HEIs with national priorities. The Framework outlines a set of strategic objective indicators of success against which institutional performance can be measured and funding can be allocated. The compacts recognise that an individual HEI is an autonomous institution with a distinctive mission, operating within a regional, national and international higher education environment, while also being part of a system and contributing to overall system performance.

The Strategic Dialogue process involves annual meetings between the executive of the HEA, supported by independent national and international experts, and the executive of the individual HEIs at which their performance compact submissions and progress against targets are discussed and assessed in detail. All HEIs have engaged seriously with this process having returned completed draft compacts setting out their mission, strategies, objectives and performance targets to 2016 under all the required headings, and within the required timescale, which was challenging (HEA, 2014a).

The first round of Strategic Dialogue concentrated on agreeing the mission, profile and strategy of each HEI, taking account of its place in the landscape, agreeing the set of strategic objectives needed to implement the strategy, agreeing a set of realistic but challenging interim and final targets associated with the achievement of these objectives, together with the indicators of success by which the HEI itself proposed that it should be measured and the clear means of verification of these indicators.

In drawing up their performance compacts, the HEIs were asked to propose the qualitative and quantitative indicators against which they wished their performance to be assessed. The compacts include the following elements:

- **Establishment of the compact:** provides for the establishment of the compact and its term, and for the HEA to inform of any actual or prospective changes to policy.
- **Performance funding framework:** sets out the performance funding framework within which the HEA will allocate performance funding.
- **Mission and strategy statement:** includes a statement of the HEI mission and strategy and also agrees to inform the HEA of any changes to its mission and profile.

- **Current and planned profile:** contains the most recent profile (as supplied by the HEA) and the planned profile 2016/17 completed by the institution itself.
- **Development plans and objectives:** sets out the HEI's development plans and objectives using standardised templates. These development plans and objectives *must* be taken from the institution's own properly formulated strategic plan. The quality of the HEI's strategic planning process will be evaluated. The areas under which objectives are sought are National Strategy objectives including:
  - regional clusters
  - participation, equal access and lifelong learning
  - teaching and learning and quality of student experience
  - high quality, internationally competitive research and innovation
  - enhanced engagement with enterprise and the community and embedded knowledge exchange
  - enhanced internationalisation
  - institutional consolidation.
- **Annual Compliance Statement:** As the Strategic Dialogue process develops, the HEA takes into account ongoing compliance of institutions, and where significant or urgent compliance issues arise, they will be discussed as part of the next Strategic Dialogue.
- **Performance Funding:** a statement of the amount of performance funding allocated.
- **Agreement:** confirmation of the agreement between the HEA and the HEI to be signed upon conclusion of the strategic dialogue process.
- **Appendices:** includes any additional material supplied by the HEI, including details of how objectives might be objectively verified.

An element of performance-related funding was introduced primarily based on the quality of the HEIs' engagement with the reformed performance governance system. As a signalling measure, a limited amount of performance funding of EUR 5 million was reserved from the allocation of the 2014 recurrent grant to HEIs to be released subject to satisfactory engagement with the Strategic Dialogue process. In the allocation of this funding the HEA was cognisant that this was the first year of Strategic Dialogue and that this was a developmental and learning stage for all involved.

In the allocation of performance funding for subsequent years, the HEA will have to consider the agreed outcomes from the current year's dialogue process. For this, each HEI will have to include not only specific objectives and indicators proposed within the compacts, but also responses to general and specific feedback given to HEIs by the HEA regarding the overall content and quality of compacts. The HEIs will be expected to demonstrate that they have incorporated any feedback into their processes for the next annual review cycle.

Moving to a system-level approach to higher education

Restructuring of the Irish higher education system has also been progressed with the aim of creating a more coherent system of mission-diverse, complementary, and highly collaborative institutions in which the diversity and areas of high quality performance that were already evident would be maintained and strengthened. The major components of restructuring are:

- The establishment of a set of Regional Clusters, the governance of which should be kept light and flexible and not dilute the accountability or autonomy of the HEIs; with strategic objectives which are clear, simple and well prioritised and focus, in the first instance, on shared academic planning and improved student pathways.

- The implementation of the recommendations of the Initial Teacher Education Review on the formation of providers of initial teacher education into six centres – through mergers and collaborations, integrating teacher education provision across all levels of education from early childhood to adult education. This process is research-led and university based.
- The establishment of a process by which consortia of IOTs that meet the requirements can apply for designation as technological universities. A core objective will, therefore, be to protect and enhance the role of the IOT sector in supporting enterprise, underpinning diversity and promoting access and participation.
- The strengthening of existing strategic alliances between HEIs in ways that protect and enhance the distinctiveness of their missions.

The Regional Cluster initiative

To aid the implementation of the National Strategy for Higher Education to 2030, Regional Clusters of HEIs were developed to assist in achieving the core objectives of a high-quality, sustainable, competitive higher education system. The aim was to build up the collective capacity, and capability of Irish higher education, to enhance quality and efficiency, to support higher education's role in the regional innovation system and, thus to strengthen international competitiveness. The HEA was responsible for steering the overall process development through the Strategic Dialogue process. Overall the response from HEIs was good given that the reorientation of internal systems and structures to take greater account of external, regional forces was both time-consuming and challenging. In total, five Regional Clusters were developed: Dublin/Leinster I, Dublin/Leinster II, West/North West, the Shannon Consortium (see Chapter 3), and the South.

The evolution of successful and sustainable regional clusters of HEIs can depend upon a symbiotic approach, encompassing, on the one hand, *inward-facing* groupings of proximate HEIs which, working together, can best optimise their collective impact in terms of effectiveness, efficiency, quality and competitiveness and, on the other hand, *outward-facing* groupings of HEIs interacting with regional agencies/external stakeholders to meet national and regional economic needs, and position the region as a self-reinforcing knowledge hub that is internationally attractive, socially beneficial, and economically successful. The further development of the Regional Clusters and the next generation of regional collaborative fora (e.g. Regional Skills Fora) are discussed in further detail in Chapter 3 of this report.

Technological universities

The National Strategy provides for the establishment of a new type of university – a technological university. Internationally, a technological university is a higher education institution that operates at the highest academic level in an environment that is specifically focused on technology and its application. A technological university is distinguished from existing universities by a mission and ethos that are faithful to and safeguard the current ethos and mission focus of the institutes of technology. These are based on career-focused higher education and on industry-focused research and innovation – this will have to be taken to a higher level in a technological university.

A technological university will also be expected to play a pivotal role in facilitating access and progression (particularly of the workforce) through strengthening existing relationships between higher education, providers of further education and training and proximate employers. In a technological university, the fields of learning will be closely related to labour market skill needs with a particular focus on programmes in science, engineering and technology and including an emphasis on workplace learning.

The mission of these new institutions "…will have a systematic focus on the preparation of graduates for complex professional roles in a changing technological world" (HEA, 2012) thus maintaining distinctiveness between universities, technological universities and institutes of technology. It will advance knowledge through research and scholarship and disseminate this knowledge to meet the needs of society and enterprise. It shall have particular regard to the needs of the region in which the university is located. Consolidation via merger is a central element of the process.

Institutes of Technology proposing to become technological universities must be able to establish that they are operating at a level equivalent to a technological university as set out in the Technological Universities Bill 2015. To date, four expressions of interest have been received by the HEA. In determining whether an application for designation as a technological university should be approved, the HEA is supported by international panels of experts who will carry out site visits and reviews as appropriate.[2]

Ireland's national innovation system

As Forfás, the former national policy advisory board for enterprise, trade, science, technology and innovation in Ireland, noted in its "Evaluation of Enterprise Supports for Research, Development and Innovation" of 2013, the country has made significant progress over the previous decade and established an international reputation in key research areas; collaboration between HEIs and industry has increased, with resulting economic benefit; and there has been an increase in business expenditure on research and development (Forfás, 2013). The report, however, also emphasised the need for continued investment in Ireland's innovation system, pointing out that it was weaker than benchmark countries such as Austria, Denmark, Sweden and Switzerland. The key challenges identified in the report were to increase the scale and depth of R&D activity in firms, to commercialise state-funded academic research, and to connect industry with HEI research and vice versa.

Innovation 2020 is Ireland's current five-year strategy for research and development, science and technology published in December 2015. It provides a whole-of-government approach to research and innovation, building on the progress made to date in the research and innovation system, addressing identified challenges, and advancing fresh strategic ideas to distinguish Ireland globally through its ability to make research work to maximum effect for the country. Its aim is to leverage a vibrant public research base in order to develop the skills base necessary to build a sustainable and resilient society, to create employment, and to establish innovative companies that will succeed internationally. A key ambition is to increase total investment in R&D in Ireland, led by the private sector, to 2.5% of gross national product. It also aims to build on existing infrastructures and achieve ambitious private-public collaborations.

Public investment in technology transfer for the period 2007-16 amounted to EUR 52 million and is focused on providing a streamlined process that delivers effective commercialisation of research (DES, 2015). Various agencies provide funding for research personnel and infrastructure, R&D activities, commercialisation and international networking. The key activities of Enterprise Ireland, Knowledge Transfer Ireland, Science Foundation Ireland, the Irish Research Council, and IDA Ireland (formerly the Industrial Development Authority), are outlined below.

Key state agencies

Enterprise Ireland

Enterprise Ireland (EI) plays a key role in the commercialisation of research. The agency provides a range of supports for both companies and research performing organisations to develop new technologies and processes that will lead to job creation and increased exports. It also has a number of supports to directly assist companies with research and innovation activities. Enterprise Ireland provides support relevant to all stages of company development, enabling companies to progress from undertaking an initial research project to higher level innovation and R&D activities. This includes in-company supports, collaboration supports, and supports for realising commercial potential (Table 1.8). Enterprise Ireland has recently published a new Strategy (Enterprise Ireland, 2017) which underlines the importance of driving innovation in Irish enterprise through new supports to reach the target of EUR 1.25 billion in R&D expenditure per annum by 2020. The Strategy emphasises the importance of innovation in the context of the Brexit decision in the UK. Implementation of the Strategy will see new innovation supports for companies and implementation of a new Innovation Toolkit to support client companies to identify innovation opportunities.

Table 1.8. **Enterprise Ireland support for research and innovation activities in higher education institutions**

In-company supports	Collaboration supports	Realising commercial potential
• **Innovative High Potential Start-Ups** encourage the establishment, and supports the development of innovation-led high potential start-up companies with a strong export focus. • **R&D Fund** provides grants to enterprise to support in-company projects which have the potential to develop novel products and services with a clear competitive advantage in their target market.	• **Innovation Vouchers** facilitate and encourage enterprises, in particular small enterprises, to engage in research or development by availing of the services available from research institutions. • **Innovation Partnerships** support joint R&D projects involving companies and research performers, where the bulk of the R&D is carried out within a third-level institute or a public research organisation. Funding is provided to the research performing body, which also receives support from the collaborating company. • **Technology Centres Programme.** These centres were developed in Irish Universities as a way of taking industry views directly into consideration when undertaking publicly funded research. • **Technology Gateways,** a network of 12 industry-focused gateways, is harnessing the innovation and technological expertise in the Institutes of Technology for the benefit of Irish industry. • **New Frontiers Programme** seeks to raise the number of business start-ups and lay the foundations for a 20% increase in the pipeline of High Potential Start-ups and other sustainable businesses, through unified course structures and rigorous processes for selecting candidates and assessing progress. • **International Collaboration** provides help, support and encouragement to Irish companies to avail of international funding for R&D.	• **Commercialisation Fund** provides support for academic researchers to bring research outputs to a point where they can be either transferred into industry or spun out into a new start-up company. • **Technology Transfer Strengthening Initiative** provides support to the ten technology transfer offices in universities and research institutions. • **Campus Incubation Centres,** in partnership with the higher education sector, promote campus entrepreneurship with the aim of commercialising the research capability in Irish universities and institutes of technology.

Source: DES (2015).

Through the Technology Transfer Strengthening Initiative (TTSI), Enterprise Ireland has invested in developing the capability and capacity for knowledge transfer and commercialisation in research performing organisations. The HEIs provide dedicated resources to knowledge transfer and commercialisation, ranging from a full technology transfer office (TTO) within a larger HEI to an individual working part-time in a smaller institution. The HEIs refer to this function in a variety of ways, such as "technology transfer", "industrial liaison", "knowledge exchange" or "innovation office", but all offer activities such as intellectual property management, licensing, partnering, consultancy and support for the creation of new companies. For the smaller IOTs, this activity is supported by the TTSI programme consortium lead partner.

Knowledge Transfer Ireland

Knowledge Transfer Ireland (KTI) was established in late 2013 as a partnership between Enterprise Ireland and the Irish Universities Association. KTI acts as a national office for technology transfer and plays a key role in the country's innovation system by providing a responsive interface between companies and the higher education system. KTI's mission is to maximise innovation from state-funded research, by getting technology, ideas and expertise into the hands of business, swiftly and easily for the benefit of the public and the economy. One of the many functions is the provision of a central hub that enables companies to explore, through a web interface, the research resources available to them throughout Ireland. KTI also has a role in allocating and managing funding to support knowledge transfer offices within Ireland's HEIs and state-funded research organisations.

Science Foundation Ireland

Science Foundation Ireland (SFI) was established in 2003 as the national foundation for investment in excellent scientific and engineering research. SFI invests in STEM academic researchers and research teams who are likely to generate new knowledge and leading-edge technologies or start up competitive enterprises. In order to fully support research prioritisation, SFI's mandate has been expanded to allow for funding the full continuum of research, applied as well as basic oriented, across all of the 14 priority research areas. SFI has several programmes that support HEI-industry relationships, including the following:

- **SFI Industry Fellowships** facilitate the placement of researchers in industry or academia to stimulate excellence through knowledge transfer and training. Fellowships enable researchers to access new technology pathways and standards, and facilitate training in the use of specialist research infrastructure.
- **SFI Partnerships** provide funding for ambitious research projects between industry and academia, enabling industry to engage with world-class academic researchers and gain access to infrastructure and intellectual property using a shared-risk funding model.
- **SFI Research Centres** consolidate the activities of public research organisations to create a critical mass of leading researchers in strategic areas. The Centres are part-funded (minimum 30%) by industry, and this ensures that there is an effective and productive partnership between academia and industry. Some 300 industry partners are involved – approximately 150 each from the multinational and indigenous sectors.
- **SFI Research Centre Spokes Programme** provides a mechanism for new industry partners to join the existing SFI Research Centres.

- **SFI Technology Innovation Development Award** provides funding to support researchers to develop entrepreneurial skills and to enable them to focus on the initial stages of developing a new or innovative technology, product, process or service with strong commercial potential. This programme, funded by SFI, is run in partnership with Enterprise Ireland.
- **SFI Academic-Led Programmes** support research, employing a broad portfolio of funding mechanisms, with the potential for economic and societal impact. Academic-led programmes, such as the SFI Investigators Programme, the SFI Future Research Leaders Award and the SFI Starting Investigator Grant address research questions and provide recruitment and career development opportunities in Ireland. SFI also provides a number of incentives to encourage applicants to apply to the European Research Council.

The Irish Research Council

The Irish Research Council (IRC) was established in 2012 from a merger of the Irish Research Council for Humanities and Social Sciences and the Irish Research Council for Science, Engineering and Technology. It operates under the aegis of the HEA. IRC operates a suite of interlinked research schemes, in particular at postgraduate and early stage postdoctoral researcher levels. IRC is responsible for funding research within and between all disciplines, and supporting the education and skills development of excellent early-stage researchers. Currently, approximately two-thirds of the IRC funding is allocated to the STEM areas. A capacity building scheme enables researchers to develop their track record and stimulate applications for European research funding, including from the European Research Council and the Horizon 2020 Societal Challenges. The IRC also has a partnership with government departments to enhance the evidence and knowledge base for a diverse range of themes. Two support programmes are directed to enhance industry mobility of early-stage researchers (Table 1.9).

Table 1.9. Irish Research Council support for industry mobility of early-stage researchers

Programme name	Description
Employment Based Postgraduate Programme	The Employment Based Postgraduate Programme provides students in all disciplines with an opportunity to work in a co-educational environment involving a higher education institution and an employment partner while at the same time gaining a masters by research or PhD qualification. Piloted in 2012, this unique programme has undergone four successive rounds of funding and is a key national mechanism (in addition to the National Research Prioritisation Exercise) for delivering on a number of objectives outlined in the national Action Plan for Jobs. Employment partners can be a business, a company, a registered charity, a social, cultural, not-for-profit, governmental or non-government organisation with a physical operational base located in Ireland that will employ the scholar for the duration of the award and provide access to facilities and expert guidance. Scholars also benefit from enhanced exposure to a commercially-oriented research environment in addition to structured postgraduate development in the academic domain. A number of national research funders are partnering with the Council on this programme. These include Enterprise Ireland, the Department of Agriculture, Food and the Marine, the Marine Institute and the Sustainable Energy Authority of Ireland.
Enterprise Partnership Scheme	Over the last decade, the Council has engaged with over 300 companies to co-fund postgraduate scholarships and postdoctoral fellowships under the Enterprise Partnership Scheme. Researchers are primarily embedded in a higher education institute, and, through close collaboration with an enterprise partner, they benefit from a rich research experience as well as having the opportunity to learn key transferable skills relevant to career formation under expert mentorship in both domains.

Source: DES (2015).

IDA Ireland

IDA Ireland plays a key role in attracting high-value R&D investments to Ireland by promoting collaboration between industry, academia, government agencies and regulatory authorities. The agency funds in-company R&D and identifies support opportunities from other funding organisations. The R&D fund provides grant-aid to clients establishing new R&D facilities, expanding existing ones, or embarking on R&D projects. The strengthening of Ireland's research ecosystem in recent years has enabled IDA Ireland to attract increased levels of high-value R&D projects, which qualitatively transform and deepen the roots of key multinational corporations in the country.

Enhancing the role of education in innovation and entrepreneurship

The 2014 National Policy Statement on Entrepreneurship in Ireland (DJEI, 2014) identified several potential roles for education institutions in supporting entrepreneurship and innovation. These include i) embedding the development of entrepreneurship in the education system across all levels of education; ii) increasing the number of professionals in information and communications technology (ICT); and iii) developing the appropriate infrastructure to support technology transfer into industry. Some of the more recent initiatives with a focus on higher education are described below and will be discussed further in Chapters 3, 4 and 5.

Engagement with enterprise and society

The HEA recently published a report on the HEI engagement activities with enterprise and society, which sets out how it aims to support implementation of the National Strategy for Higher Education to 2030 and the system-wide reform and development programme (HEA, 2015). The aim is to organise a step-change in the scale and quality of partnerships between higher education and the enterprise community in all regions of the country. It builds on a range of initiatives and practices that are already in place between higher education and enterprise, targeted national talent development initiatives and several local and regional partnerships between education providers and individual companies. Implementation of this engagement strategy has been incorporated into the implementation of the National Skills Strategy (DES 2016) which has a strong focus on entrepreneurship and employer participation in the development of skills.

Labour market activation initiatives

Aside from standard entry routes to higher education, there has been an increased focus in recent years on labour market activation programmes that are directly linked to enterprise and industry needs. Examples include the ICT Skills Action Plan and the Springboard Programme, both of which are administered by the HEA on behalf of the DES.

The first ICT Skills Action Plan was published in 2012 as a collaborative industry-government approach to increasing the domestic supply of high-level ICT graduates. The latest plan includes an ambition to make Ireland a global leader for ICT talent and skills, with the education system satisfying 74% of the forecast industry demand for high-level ICT skills by 2018 (up from the current level, estimated at over 60%). An updated ICT Skills Action Plan is expected to be published in 2017.

To address the emerging skills gaps, the current Plan's key targets include doubling the output of Level 8 graduates by 2018 and interim steps to increase supply through conversion and reskilling programmes. Significant progress has been made in meeting these targets. The Plan also includes measures to attract highly skilled ICT professionals from abroad to augment the domestic supply. These measures include streamlining the operation of the employment permit regime and promoting Ireland as a destination for skilled ICT professionals. Industry's continued upskilling and development of its current employees will also make a vital contribution to the achievement of the Plan's goals.

The Springboard+ Programme is a recent labour market activation initiative administered by the HEA on behalf of the DES. It provides recently unemployed people with free higher education opportunities, giving them the opportunity to reskill and return to work. Springboard+ courses are provided in areas identified as those where there is a shortage of skills and/or strong growth leading to potential skills shortages. Each course aims to cross-skill or up-skill participants to enable them to restart their careers, and to provide a pipeline of graduates for enterprise sectors that are growing and expanding. The Springboard Programme has been running since 2011 and was renamed Springboard+ in 2014 and saw the incorporation of a standalone ICT Skills Conversion programme under the Springboard branding. The full-time ICT Conversion programmes have been open to all applicants regardless of employment status. In 2016, a new part-time ICT Conversion programme was introduced as part of the Springboard+ 2016 call. Over 30 000 people have completed courses to date with an average of 6 000 free places available per academic year. Over 90% of the 2015/16 courses (excluding entrepreneurship courses) include work placements, and employers see such work experience as a useful complement to course studies. The HEA has built a rigorous evaluation framework into the initiative, including publishing process evaluations and reporting on outcomes to date. Three comprehensive evaluations of outcomes have been published to date, with participants and graduates, with the HEIs involved, and with enterprise (HEA, 2017b). The evaluations show that, within two years of completing a course, 60% of graduates are back in employment or self-employment.

Action Plans for Jobs

Since 2012, a series of Action Plans for Jobs has acted as key policy instrument to supporting job creation and enterprise growth. Each year, these documents set out a series of commitments to be delivered under a number of thematic headings. So far, over 1 000 actions have been implemented and the original target to support the creation of 100 000 new jobs by 2016 has been exceeded with nearly 190 000 more people now at work.[3] Actions to align skills provision with the needs of enterprise have been a feature of every plan so far.

Building on the success of the national Action Plans for Jobs, a series of eight regional Action Plans for Jobs was developed in 2015 with the aim of distributing job creation more evenly across the country for the period 2015-17. Both the national and the regional Action Plans have been developed with extensive stakeholder consultation, including engagement with state agencies, local government, education providers (both further and higher education), industry, and business representatives (DJEI, 2017).

The National Skills Strategy and Regional Skills Fora

The Department of Education and Skills has developed the National Skills Strategy 2025 (DES, 2016). The purpose is to provide a framework for skills development that will help drive Ireland's growth both economically and societally over the next decade. It sets out a wide range of actions under six key objectives, aimed at improving the development, supply and use of skills over the next decade.

The National Skills Strategy also provides for the establishment of the National Skills Council that will oversee research, forecasting and prioritisation of skills needs in the economy, and nine so-called Regional Skills Fora, which bring together employers and the education and training system in each region to facilitate the planning and delivery of programmes, to reduce duplication, and to inform national funding decisions. The Regional Skills Fora have been effective in raising the awareness of the range of programmes on offer across a region and how these can be accessed.

Developing entrepreneurial mindsets

There is a joint understanding and commitment across all policy makers that manifestations of entrepreneurial mindsets in the form of enterprise[4] and entrepreneurship are crucial for addressing broader policy objectives through innovation and partnership – tackling grand global challenges, such as sustainable energy, healthy ageing and smart cities (DJEI, 2015b; DES, 2016). The National Skills Strategy provides for the completion of an Entrepreneurship Education Policy Statement that will inform the development of entrepreneurship education guidelines for schools. It also provides for the pilot and support of Makerspaces, Fab labs and innovative summer camp ideas to promote entrepreneurial thinking, STEM and design skills amongst secondary school students.

National networks to enhance enterprise and entrepreneurship in higher education

Recently, several networks have been forming across the Irish HEIs to promote and develop enterprise and entrepreneurship. CEEN, the Campus Entrepreneurship Enterprise Network, is one of them. CEEN aims to create a sustainable national platform for raising the profile of entrepreneurship, extending engagement and further developing entrepreneurship across Irish HEIs. It will do this by providing a vehicle for a national dialogue between academia, industry and voluntary and public sectors on the development of entrepreneurship education, promoting excellence in the field by stimulating research, developing new pedagogy, evaluating and disseminating good practice initiatives, and facilitating the networking and collaboration within and between HEIs. Examples of CEEN's projects include the National Educators Programme, the Engaged Student Project, Entrepreneurship Scholarship Scheme, and the Spark Social Enterprise Awards (CEEN, 2017).

Entrepreneurship education activities in Irish HEIs

Most HEIs in Ireland are targeting a very significant development and embedding of entrepreneurship education in programmes at both undergraduate and at postgraduate level. Table 1.10 gives an overview of current initiatives which were included in the institutional compacts presented in 2016.

Table 1.10. **Entrepreneurship education activities in the institutional compacts of Irish higher education institutions (2016)**

Institution(s)	Details
University College Dublin, Trinity College Dublin	Provision for entrepreneurship jointly through the Innovation Academy; both are committed to mainstreaming entrepreneurship into the wider student experience.
University College of Cork (UCC)	UCC is planning to have an entrepreneurship component available to all programmes by 2016.
Institute of Technology Tralee	The Centre for Entrepreneurship Education Development targets all aspects of entrepreneurship and embeds it across the Institute. The Institute has an emphasis on researcher entrepreneurship and at present has particular emphasis on the food industry and on intergenerational entrepreneurs.
Galway-Mayo Institute of Technology	In GMIT, employability, including entrepreneurship, is identified as a key driver of its teaching and learning strategy; and GMIT aims to have an entrepreneurship module provided to all students by 2016.
Dublin Institute of Technology	Entrepreneurial skills and competence is a core part of the mission, vision and values of DIT, and these inform its research strategy. DIT has a formal objective to include an entrepreneurship module in 30% of programmes.
Cork Institute of Technology (CIT)	CIT treats entrepreneurial skill as a core graduate attribute which it aims for all CIT graduates to have.
Dún Laoghaire Institute of Art, Design and Technology (IADT)	IADT recognises that a high proportion of its graduates will be employed as sole trading entrepreneurs and seeks to embed preparation for this in its programmes; regionally it is focused on provision of entrepreneurship education for the creative industries.
Tallaght Institute of Technology	IT Tallaght has student entrepreneurship awards from its incubation centre.
National University of Ireland, Galway (NUIG)	A core principle of NUIG's research strategy is that research should be entrepreneurial.
University of Limerick	Junior entrepreneurship programme in Shannon consortium. Entrepreneurial Research Culture.
National College of Art & Design, Dublin (NCAD)	NCAD has restructured all of its undergraduate programmes to provide an emphasis on generic skills including entrepreneurship.
Letterkenny Institute of Technology, Institute of Technology Sligo, Galway-Mayo Institute of Technology	These institutions have agreed regional entrepreneurship education programmes linked to three incubation centres.
Regional Cluster: Dublin City University, Athlone Institute of Technology, Dundalk Institute of Technology, DKIT, National University of Ireland, Maynooth	Dublin Leinster Pillar 2 regional cluster is planning a co-ordinated regional approach to the development of student entrepreneurship.
Technological universities	Entrepreneurship education features strongly in the vision for the new proposed technological universities.

Source: Higher Education Authority (2014a).

Notes

1. An association of private for-profit providers, the Higher Education Colleges Association (HECA, *www.heca.ie*) has a list of affiliated members on its website, but this is not an exhaustive list.

2. The designation process consists of four stages as follows: i) expression of interest; ii) preparation of a plan to meet the criteria; iii) evaluation of the plan, iv) an application for designation.

3. The Action Plan for Jobs 2012 included an ambition to create 100 000 jobs by 2016.

4. Enterprise here refers to entrepreneurial skills in the broader sense which are also important for developing skills in the future workforce to ensure they make the maximum contribution to productivity and growth in public, private and third sector organisations.

References

CEEN (2017), "Campus Entrepreneurship Enterprise Network" website, *www.ceen.ie/* (accessed 11 February 2017).

Department of Education and Skills (2011), *National Strategy for Higher Education to 2030*, published online, *www.hea.ie/sites/default/files/national_strategy_for_higher_education_2030.pdf* (accessed 11 February 2017).

Department of Education and Skills (2015), *Country Background Report Ireland*, prepared for the HEInnovate Ireland country review, unpublished report submitted to the OECD.

Department for Education and Skills (2016), *National Skills Strategy 2025 – Ireland's Future*, published online, *www.education.ie/en/Publications/Policy-Reports/pub_national_skills_strategy_2025.pdf* (accessed 11 February 2017).

Department of Enterprise, Jobs and Innovation (2013), *Survey of Research & Development in the Higher Education Sector 2012/2013*, published online, *www.djei.ie/en/Publications/Publication-files/Survey-of-Research-and-Development-in-the-Higher-Education-Sector-2012-2013.pdf* (accessed 11 February 2017).

Department of Enterprise, Jobs and Innovation (2014), *National Policy Statement on Entrepreneurship in Ireland*, published online, *www.localenterprise.ie/Documents-and-Publications/Entrepreneurship-in-Ireland-2014.pdf* (accessed 11 February 2017).

Department for Jobs, Enterprise and Innovation (2015a), *Survey of Research & Development in the Higher Education Sector 2012/2013*, published online, *www.djei.ie/en/Publications/Publication-files/Survey-of-Research-and-Development-in-the-Higher-Education-Sector-2012-2013.pdf* (accessed 11 February 2017).

Department of Enterprise, Jobs and Innovation (2015b), *Enterprise 2025 – Ireland's National Enterprise Policy 2015-2025*, published online, *www.djei.ie/en/Publications/Publication-files/Enterprise-2025-Summary-Report.pdf* (accessed 11 February 2017).

Department of Enterprise, Jobs and Innovation (2016), *Inspiring Partnership – The National IP Protocol 2016. Policies and resources to help industry make good use of public research in Ireland*, published online, *www.knowledgetransferireland.com/ManagingIP/KTI-Protocol-2016.pdf* (accessed 11 February 2017).

Department of Enterprise, Jobs and Innovation (2017), "Action Plan for Jobs" website, *www.actionplanforjobs.ie/* (accessed 11 February 2017).

Enterprise Ireland (2016), *Strategy 2017-2020*, published online, *https://enterprise-ireland.com/en/Publications/Reports-Published-Strategies/Strategy-2017-to-2020.pdf*, (accessed 11 February 2017).

European University Association (2013), *Financially Sustainable Universities. Full Costing: Progress and Practice*, EUA Publishing, Brussels.

Forfás (2013), *Evaluation of Enterprise Supports for Research, Development and Innovation*, published online, *www.djei.ie/en/Publications/Publication-files/Forf%C3%A1s/Evaluation-of-Enterprise-Supports-for-Research-Development-and-Innovation.pdf* (accessed 11 February 2017).

Higher Education Authority (2012), *Towards a Future Higher Education Landscape*, published online, *www.9thlevel.ie/wp-content/uploads/TowardsaFutureHigherEducationLandscape.pdf* (accessed 11 February 2017).

Higher Education Authority (2014a), *Higher Education System Performance. First Report 2014-2016. Report of the Higher Education Authority to the Minister for Education and Skills*, published online, *www.education.ie/en/Publications/Education-Reports/Higher-Education-System-Performance-First-report-2014-2016.pdf* (accessed 11 February 2017).

Higher Education Authority (2014b), *Review of Workload Allocation Models in Irish Higher Education Institutions*, Higher Education Authority, Dublin.

Higher Education Authority (2015), *Collaborating for Talent and Growth: Strategy for Higher Education – Enterprise Engagement 2015-2020*, published online, *www.hea.ie/sites/default/files/hea_collaborating_for_talent_and_growth_strategy_he-enterprise_june_2015.pdf* (accessed 11 February 2017).

Higher Education Authority (2016a), *Investing in National Ambition: A Strategy for Funding Higher Education. Report of the expert group on future funding for higher education*, published online, *www.education.ie/en/Publications/Policy-Reports/Investing-in-National-Ambition-A-Strategy-for-Funding-Higher-Education.pdf*,(accessed 11 February 2017).

Higher Education Authority (2016b), Financial Review of the Institutes of Technology, published online, *www.hea.ie/sites/default/files/final_iot_financial_review_3_11.pdf* (accessed 11 February 2017).

Higher Education Authority Ireland (2017a), "Student enrolment numbers" website, *www.hea.ie/node/1557* (accessed 11 February 2017).

Higher Education Authority (2017b), "Springboard Programme" website, *www.springboardcourses.ie* (accessed 11 February 2017).

Chapter 2

Applying HEInnovate to higher education in Ireland

> This chapter provides a holistic assessment of entrepreneurship and innovation in the Irish higher education system using the seven dimensions and 37 statements of the European Commission-OECD HEInnovate framework. It includes discussion of strategy, governance and resources, practices in organising education, research and engagement with business and society, and measuring impact. The analysis is based on study visits to six institutions and the results of a system-wide HEI Leader Survey. The Chapter concludes with a presentation of the key recommendations resulting from the Irish HEInnovate country review.

HEInnovate describes the innovative and entrepreneurial HEI as "designed to empower students and staff to demonstrate enterprise, innovation and creativity in teaching, research, and engagement with business and society. Its activities are directed to enhance learning, knowledge production and exchange in a highly complex and changing societal environment; and are dedicated to create public value via processes of open engagement". How this can be translated into daily practice in HEIs, is described through 37 statements which are organised in seven dimensions. In the following, key findings from applying the HEInnovate guiding framework to HEIs in Ireland are presented. The information is based on the results of the HEI Leaders Survey in Ireland and information from detailed interviews with stakeholders in the case study HEIs.

Leadership and governance

Entrepreneurship is a major part of the strategy of the higher education institution

Supporting entrepreneurship through higher education is a policy priority in Ireland (see Chapter 1). Approximately two-thirds of the surveyed higher education institutions (HEIs) have agreements with government bodies related to the entrepreneurship education activities they offer, and more than half for start-up support measures. Strategies supporting knowledge exchange, entrepreneurship and innovation are well evolved, understood and being implemented through various activities including strategic planning processes at institutional and unit levels. This provides a fertile environment not only for learner development and the commercialisation of research but also for the creation of new transdisciplinary research areas which will be crucial to effectively addressing the emerging societal challenges of the 21st century.

All of the six HEIs visited clearly demonstrated the embedding of entrepreneurship within their institute strategy[1] and across the organisation as a whole. Dedicated and professional entrepreneurship teams have introduced new initiatives and brought in international partners. Entrepreneurship education is fully backed by senior management. Presidents awards dedicated to entrepreneurship and innovation are used as effective initiatives to recognise and reward students and staff for their achievements.

Figure 2.1 shows the varying entrepreneurship related objectives of Irish HEIs derived from the HEI Leader Survey implemented as part of this review. In common is the desire of HEIs to help students develop entrepreneurial competences and skills. Promoting self-employment and business start-up as viable career options to students was perceived as slightly more important by the institutes of technology (IOTs). Both universities and IOTs consider themselves as having a leading role in the local development agenda and in co-operating with local firms. A notable difference exists with regard to generating revenue from spin-off activities and the commercialisation of research results: universities saw this as having a greater importance than IOTs.

Figure 2.1. **Entrepreneurship objectives of Irish higher education institutions**

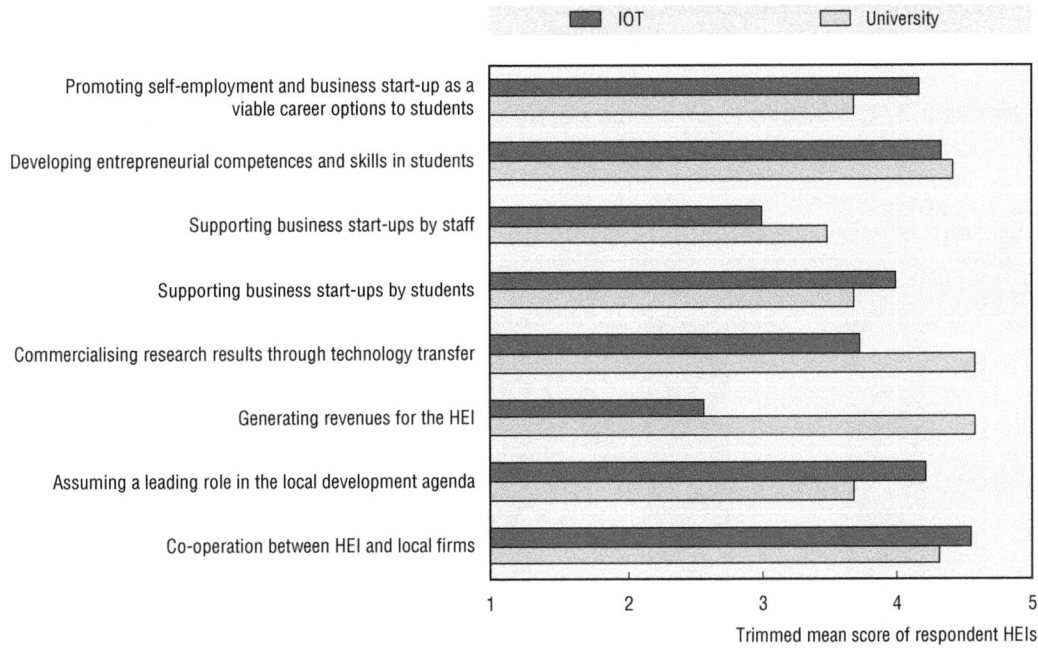

Notes: Higher education institutions (HEIs) were asked: "How important are the following objectives for your HEI?". Respondents indicated the level of importance on a 5-point Likert scale from 1 ="Not important at all to 5 ="Very important". 5% trimmed means are shown. The total number of responses was 17, of which 7 were from universities and 10 from institutes of technology (IOT). The overall survey response rate was 81%. The survey response rates per HEI type are the following: universities (100%), institutes of technology (71%).
Source: OECD HEI Leader Survey Ireland (2015).

There is commitment at a high level to implementing the entrepreneurial agenda

An effective and sustainable implementation of the entrepreneurial agenda requires a high level of commitment. The starting point is building a shared understanding of what the entrepreneurial agenda means for the different stakeholders in the HEI, that is, leadership, academic staff, administrative staff and students, and for external partners (e.g. government, businesses, civil society organisations, donors). Central to this are communication and consultation about what the entrepreneurial agenda entails in terms of objectives, activities, priorities and resources. This can be linked with the process of defining and reviewing the HEI strategy. All surveyed HEIs reported involving staff in consultations and 80% reported involving students. Half of the HEIs consult local and regional governments as well as local businesses and their representative bodies, and slightly less (45%) reach out to multinational corporations.

There is no doubt that the Irish higher education system as a whole values the importance of developing awareness of entrepreneurship, and actively encourages individuals to develop the attitudes, skills and knowledge to become entrepreneurs. Most of the HEIs surveyed offer entrepreneurship education activities, which aim at competence development (85%), and targeted start-up support measures (80%). More than half of the HEIs have created top-level management positions to support these activities in addition to positions at departmental/faculty level.

According to the HEI Leader Survey, on average one-third of students currently participate in entrepreneurship education activities, and the HEIs expect this to rise to 50% in the next five years. To increase participation rates and the offer of entrepreneurship education activities, a range of targeted efforts are underway (Figure 2.2). The most common measures to enhance participation are communication efforts, invitation of entrepreneurs as guest speakers, and business plan competitions with attractive prizes.

Figure 2.2. **Measures to enhance participation in entrepreneurship education**

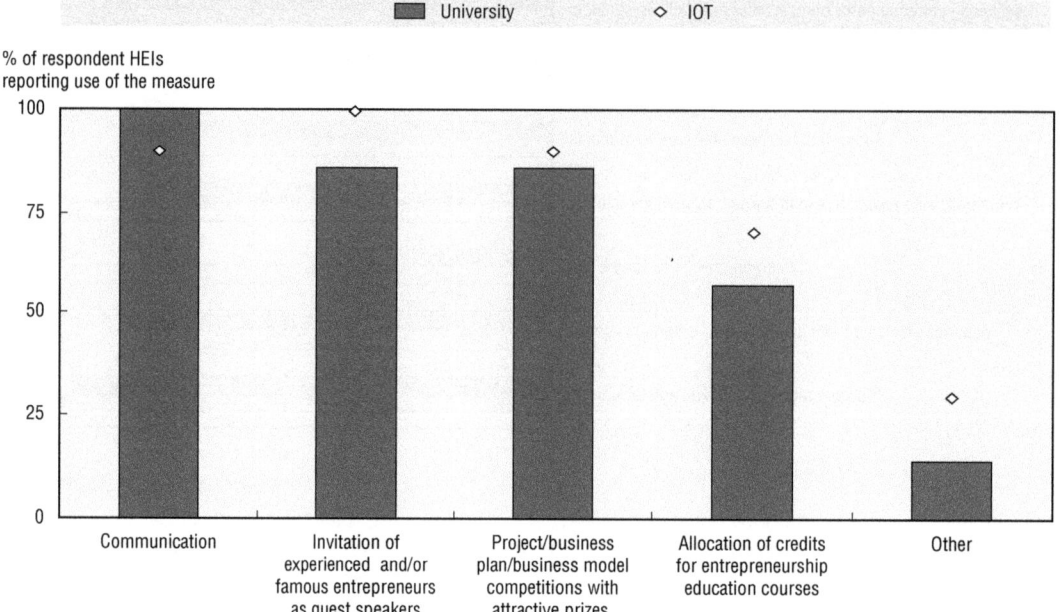

Notes: Higher education institutions (HEIs) were asked: "What measures does your HEI implement to increase participation rates in entrepreneurship education activities?". The total number of responses was 17, of which 7 were from universities and 10 from institutes of technology (IOT). The overall survey response rate was 81%. The survey response rates per HEI type are the following: universities (100%), institutes of technology (71%).
Source: OECD HEI Leader Survey Ireland (2015).

Only 60% reported using the allocation of credits to raise participation rates in line with the European Credit Transfer and Accumulation System (ECTS). This, however, could be a very effective way of raising the interest of students. IOTs appear to be more active than universities in this regard in raising the take-up of entrepreneurship education activities overall.

There is a model in place for co-ordinating and integrating entrepreneurial activities across the HEI

HEIs across Europe have experimented with different approaches to establishing an effective model for co-ordinating and integrating various entrepreneurial activities across the institution, and to facilitate exchange of experiences and peer-support, particularly in education activities. A common approach is to anchor the entrepreneurial agenda within senior management, often in the form of a dedicated unit, which is part of the Rector's/President's or the Vice-Rector's/Vice-President's office. Another approach is to appoint a number of professors who have entrepreneurship in their title or a chair in entrepreneurship. An increasingly practiced approach is the establishment of an entrepreneurship centre to ensure easy access and visibility inside and outside the HEI. Whichever model is employed, it should take into account and build on existing relationships both inside the HEI and in the surrounding entrepreneurship ecosystem.

Examples of all three approaches are present in Irish HEIs. The entrepreneurial agenda is supported and driven at senior management level most usually by a combination of the Vice-President for Research and the heads of faculty. Below this level no consistent model is imposed, which reflects the innovative and bottom-up approach taken by HEIs to deliver entrepreneurship and innovation development. All surveyed HEIs reported that they have a permanent contact point (e.g. entrepreneurship centre) where individuals or teams, who would like to start up a business can go for support. With the exception of one respondent, these centres were an integral part of the HEI.

The HEI encourages and supports faculties and units to act entrepreneurially

Individual faculties and units in all of the HEIs visited clearly demonstrated an ability to develop faculty initiatives in both innovation and entrepreneurship relevant to local, regional, national and in some instances international needs. This reflects well in terms of the ability of Irish HEIs to be flexible and responsive within individual disciplines and at different levels within their organisational structure in order to meet the needs of both internal and external stakeholders. National competitions, such as the all-Ireland business plan competition, are seen as very important to showcase achievements within HEIs.

The HEI is a driving force for entrepreneurship and innovation in regional, social and community development

Irish HEIs, especially in a regional context, are important actors in the social and economic development of the local area. In some instances they might be the sole higher education provider in a region (which is very critical in a country like Ireland where student mobility is so low), and often they are also one of the largest employers and purchasers of goods and services. Based on the meetings conducted with external stakeholders, including state agencies responsible for industry and enterprise support, research and development, business and industry groups and local authority representatives, the HEIs are seen as key drivers for innovation and entrepreneurship in the wider regional, social and community environment.

The HEIs visited have embedded academic expertise in local and regional development, capacity building, organisational development etc. within their own institutions. This practice was observed not only in the areas of Science, Technology, Engineering and Mathematics (STEM) but also in the Arts, Humanities and Social Sciences (AHSS). Several examples of good and promising practice are discussed in Chapter 5.

The HEI Leader Survey indicates that the HEIs have developed relationships with various public and non-public bodies for the purposes of contributing to local development (Figure 2.3). The surveyed IOTs appear to be more connected with local strategic partnerships and industry clusters than the universities. Also, collaboration with regional and local government bodies and national government agencies appears to be more developed in IOTs than in universities.

Figure 2.3. **Strategic local development partners of Irish higher education institutions**

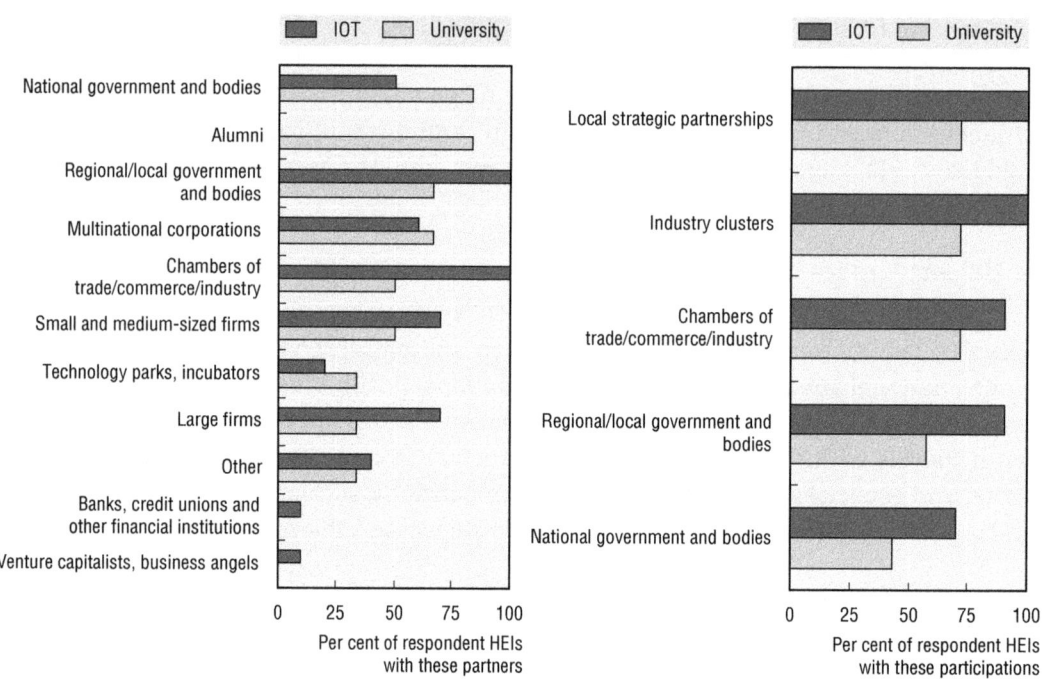

Notes: The chart on the left shows the involvement of external stakeholders in the governing bodies of Irish higher education institutions (HEIs). Respondents were asked "Which of the following organisations or individuals are members of the governing board of your HEI?". The total number of responses analysed was 16, of which 6 were universities and 10 institutes of technology (IOT). The chart on the right shows the involvement of HEIs in governing boards or strategic positions of external stakeholders. Respondents were asked "Does your HEI participate in the governing boards of the following organisations and strategic initiatives to define the development directions of the surrounding local economy?". 17 HEIs responded to this question, of which 7 were universities and 10 institutes of technology (IOT). The overall survey response rate was 81%. The survey response rates per HEI type are the following: universities (100%), institutes of technology (71%).
Source: OECD HEI Leader Survey Ireland (2015).

Organisational capacity: Funding, people and incentives

Entrepreneurial objectives are supported by a wide range of sustainable funding and investment sources

Irish HEIs are heavily, and in some cases almost totally, dependent on contract rather than core funding to support entrepreneurial and innovation activities including R&D, enterprise support and new teaching and learning initiatives. This position has become even more pronounced during the recent economic crisis, which has seen a significant reduction in state funding for the higher education system. This is impacting on the sustainability of the HEIs' entrepreneurial and innovation strategies as their financial strategies have to be fluid and flexible and focused on maintaining core activities principally in the teaching and learning arena.

Nevertheless, HEIs have responded very positively in terms of securing additional sources of funding or increasing their share of external funding sources. Notable is their continued commitment to prioritise entrepreneurial and innovation activities due to their positive local development impact. Figure 2.4 shows the HEI Leader Survey results relevant to current and expected sources of funding for entrepreneurship support, including both education and start-up support activities. The largest source of funding comes from project-specific grants from national government, 30% is from the HEI's regular budget and slightly

Figure 2.4. **Financing entrepreneurship support in Irish higher education institutions**

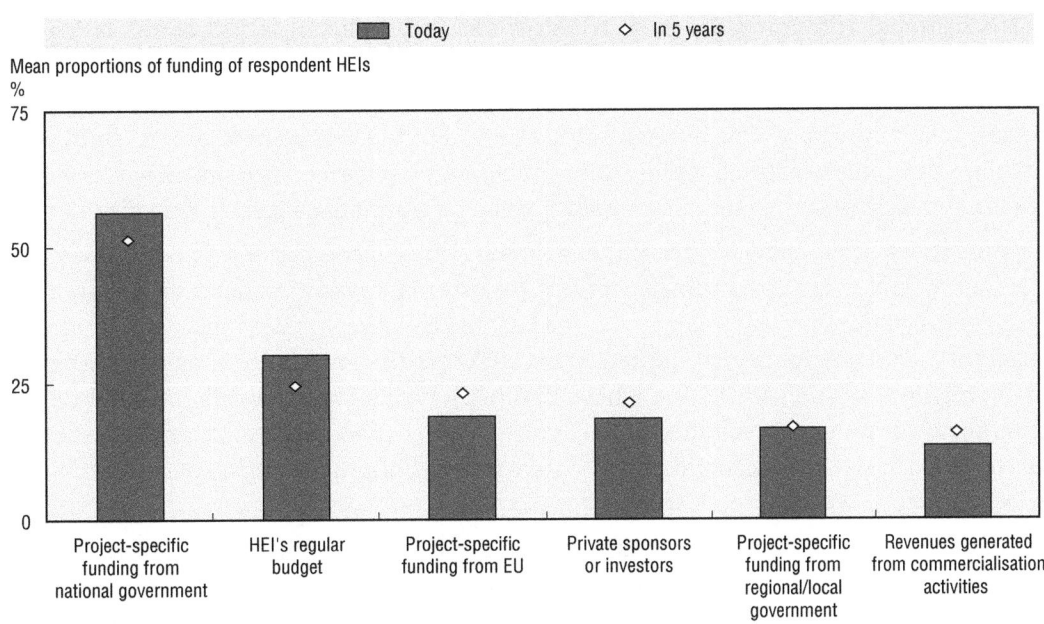

Notes: Higher education institutions (HEIs) that currently offer entrepreneurship support were asked "What is the approximate ratio of the different funding sources your higher education institution uses to finance the entrepreneurship support activities?", and "Looking ahead for five years what ratio do you expect to come from the following sources for financing these activities?". The total number of responses was 17, of which 7 were from universities and 10 from institutes of technology (IOT). The overall survey response rate was 81%. The survey response rates per HEI type are the following: universities (100%), institutes of technology (71%).
Source: OECD HEI Leader Survey Ireland (2015).

below 20% are project-specific funding from the European Union (EU), private sponsors or investors, and funding from regional or local governments. Revenues generated from commercialisation activities fund approximately 13% of the entrepreneurship support activities. Looking five years ahead, the HEIs expect to see an increase in funding from the EU, private sources and revenues from commercialisation activities, whereas funding from national government and HEI budgets are expected to decrease.

The HEI has the capacity and culture to build new relationships and synergies across the institution

In general, communication and collaboration between faculties, students and academic staff appears to take place through both formal and informal channels. Many examples of inter-faculty and inter-disciplinary collaborations were observed during the study visits, including formal agreements for academic staff to teach entrepreneurship in other faculties.

Support staff who can help spot opportunities and engineer the interdisciplinary and external partnerships that are increasingly needed to secure research funding have become a rare luxury. In many cases it is down to individual researchers to build the partnerships needed and write proposals. In the IOTs this is hugely challenging given the high teaching load during term time. Where support staff are in place they seem to spend a high proportion of their time educating themselves about requirements within the funding organisations and disseminating this information to the research community.

Collaboration of HEIs, for example in the Regional Clusters and Regional Skills Fora, is an important feature of the Irish higher education system as will be discussed further in Chapter 3.

The HEI is open to engaging and recruiting individuals with entrepreneurial attitudes, behaviour and experience

Institutional autonomy is a core principle of higher education in Ireland as it is in many other countries. Reduced funding with increased rules and conditionality has meant that while the principle of autonomy remains, in practice HEIs have far less flexibility and freedom than in the past. This is particularly relevant to the recruitment of new staff, with HEIs having to comply with nationally determined employment control frameworks which have limited their ability to recruit new staff of the appropriate calibre and quality.

Another aspect of knowledge links, experience, and new sources of revenue is related to academic consultancy, i.e. academics working for external organisations in their own time. When these activities remain unknown to the HEI, the benefits and the impacts of academic consultancy work are not being captured or fed back into the knowledge activities of the HEI and the higher education sector as a whole. In other jurisdictions arrangements are in place which allow academic consultancy be recognised rather than operate on an ad-hoc basis which enables the HEI, the academic and the state to benefit from the impact of such activities.

The National Strategy for Higher Education (see Chapter 1), has been a major step towards supporting HEIs in their efforts to enhance entrepreneurship and innovation. When academic staff are recruited or promoted, their innovation and entrepreneurship activities and outcomes are taken into account (e.g. considering patents and patent licensing agreements, contract research and development with companies or other organisations, spin-off creation, participations in non-governmental organisation (NGO) activities that contribute to local development or triple/quadruple helix models of collaboration, teaching and learning activities, acting as a mentor to student entrepreneurs, etc.). Highly qualified professionals who are fully dedicated to innovation and entrepreneurship activities have well-defined and relatively stable careers within the HEI as their salaries are partly funded from the HEI's budget and not only from project-based funding. This ensures that people with relevant knowledge and skills remain in such functions and at the HEI or in the higher education sector.

The HEI invests in staff development to support its entrepreneurial agenda

A strong emphasis is placed on teaching and learning practices within staff development programmes in the Irish higher education system. Most, if not all, HEIs offer courses in teaching and learning practice to their academic staff. The National Forum for the Enhancement of Teaching and Learning in Higher Education is a platform that has great potential to introduce and enhance innovative pedagogies and teaching methods through rewards and guidance. 140 discipline groups exist and a collaborative website enhances cross-discipline exchange. It will be important that the Forum provides enough space (e.g. working groups) to include existing networks, such as the Campus Entrepreneurship Enterprise Network (CEEN) and others to build on already existing good practice and to ensure the sustainability of networks, which have been formed in the past (see Chapter 1 for more information on CEEN). The National Forum has recently published a national approach to continuous professional development, which is currently being piloted.

Incentives and rewards are given to staff who actively support the entrepreneurial agenda

Ensuring the success of engagement and outreach activities requires resources, which are made available on a long-term basis and are integrated into the wider resource development and incentive system. Current pay structures and employment conditions within the Irish higher education system do not allow for bonus payments or other financial rewards for those who actively support the HEI's entrepreneurial agenda. Individual HEIs, however, do provide other incentives including a reduction in teaching loads, in support of, for example, research and development (R&D) activities, and awards schemes for staff who demonstrate excellence in teaching and learning and in some HEIs' entrepreneurial activity. Less common are rewards for mentoring nascent entrepreneurs. Staff rewards, in general, seem to be more common in universities than in IOTs (Figure 2.5).

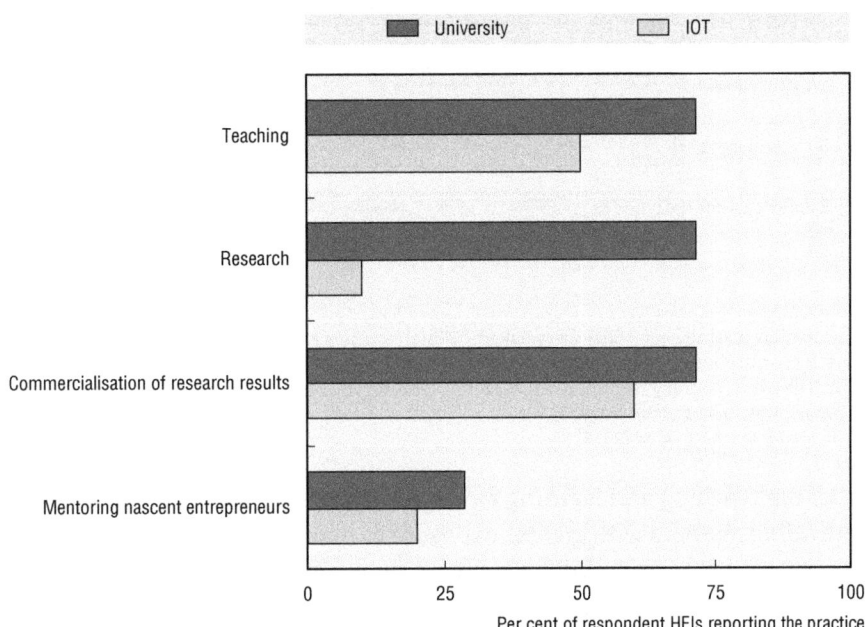

Figure 2.5. **Rewarding excellent performance in Irish higher education institutions**

Notes: Higher education institutions (HEIs) were asked: "Are there formalised processes to identify and reward excellent performance in teaching?", "Are there formalised processes to identify and reward excellent performance in research?", "Does your HEI have an incentive system for staff, who actively support the commercialisation of research for example by making research results available, acting as mentors, etc.?". The total number of responses was 17, of which 7 were from universities and 10 from institutes of technology (IOT). The overall survey response rate was 81%. The survey response rates per HEI type are the following: universities (100%), institutes of technology (71%).
Source: OECD HEI Leader Survey Ireland (2015).

Entrepreneurial teaching and learning

The HEI provides diverse formal learning opportunities to develop entrepreneurial mindsets and skills

Stimulating entrepreneurship plays an important role in Irish higher education and entrepreneurship education is offered across the sector in various formats and across many disciplines. In all the HEIs visited for this report, there was clear evidence of the centrality of student development in the mission of the institutions and the desire to help students develop entrepreneurial mindset and behaviours. Course modules and programmes in entrepreneurship commonly originated from the HEI's business school. Increasingly these have been adapted and transferred into other disciplines and in some cases adopted across multiple disciplines within HEIs.

Figure 2.6 shows the target groups of entrepreneurship education activities. It is clear that while all HEIs target Level 7 (Ordinary Bachelor) and Level 8 (Bachelor) students, universities focus more on postgraduate programmes than the IOTs. Students in lifelong learning programmes are not yet a common target group.[2]

Figure 2.6. **Target groups of entrepreneurship education activities in Irish HEIs**

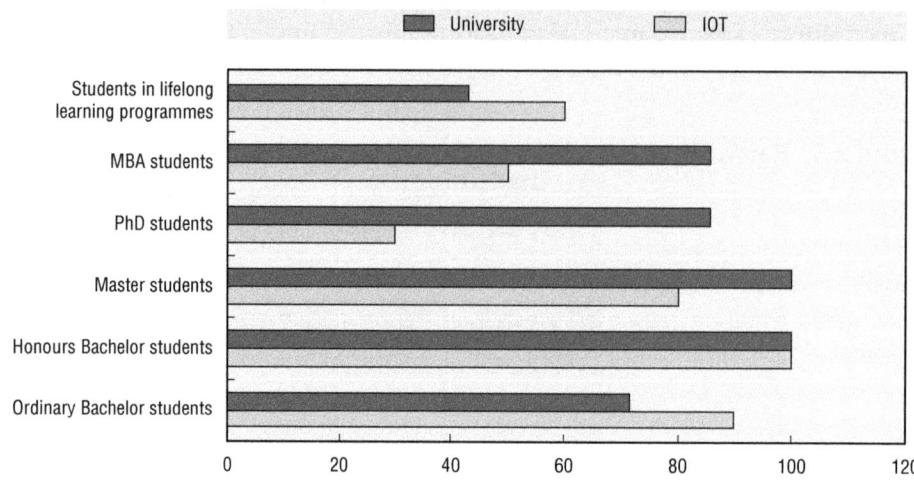

Per cent of respondent HEIs reporting the practice

Notes: Higher education institutions (HEIs) were asked: "Which are target groups of the entrepreneurship education activities?". The total number of responses was 17, of which 7 were from universities and 10 from institutes of technology (IOT). The overall survey response rate was 81%. The survey response rates per HEI type are the following: universities (100%), institutes of technology (71%).
Source: OECD HEI Leader Survey Ireland (2015).

As part of the teaching and learning strategies in HEIs, an increasing emphasis is being placed on providing learners with greater exposure to real world experiences which promote entrepreneurial mindset and skills through live projects and case studies as well as expanded work placement programmes. Methods used to deliver the programmes are also varied and include classroom delivery, one-to-one mentoring, peer mentoring and group work, use of live projects, case studies and hackathons. The HEI Leader Survey shows that a wide range of teaching methods are used across the different study programmes, including problem-based learning, internships, visits to companies, tutoring, and self-learning exercises using digital learning environments. Less common are the use of Massive Open Online Courses (MOOCs) and online lectures (Figure 2.7).

Looking more specifically at entrepreneurship education, lectures and frontal teaching are the most common teaching methods, followed by entrepreneurs as guest speakers in class and project-based learning. Comparing the teaching approaches in entrepreneurship education activities with all education activities, not much difference can be noted for frontal teaching, whereas problem-based learning, visits to companies and digital learning environments seem to be practiced less often in entrepreneurship education activities. Experience reports by start-ups are common or regularly organised in less than half of the HEIs which currently offer entrepreneurship education activities (Figure 2.8).

The HEI provides diverse informal learning opportunities and experiences to stimulate the development of entrepreneurial mindsets and skills

Extra-curricular learning opportunities have become an important complement to formal entrepreneurship courses. A very popular informal learning method with students is

Figure 2.7. **Teaching methods in Irish higher education**

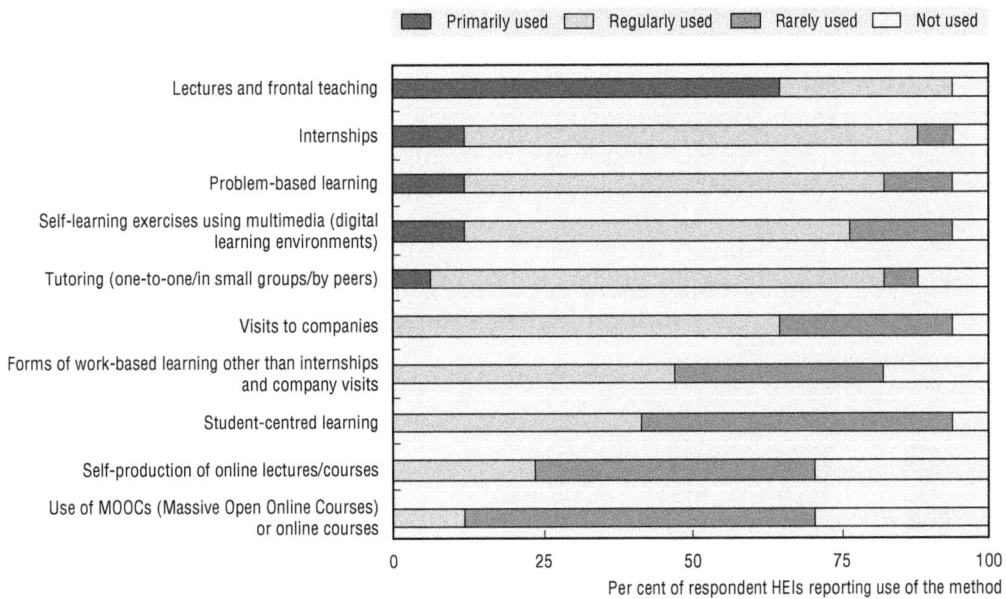

Notes: Higher education institutions (HEIs) were asked: "To what extent are the following teaching methods used at your HEI?". Response options were "not used", "rarely used", "regularly used", "primarily used". A total of 17 HEIs responded (7 universities, 10 institutes of technology). The overall survey response rate was 81%. The survey response rates per HEI type are the following: universities (100%), institutes of technology (71%).
Source: OECD HEI Leader Survey Ireland (2015).

Figure 2.8. **Teaching methods in entrepreneurship courses in Irish higher education**

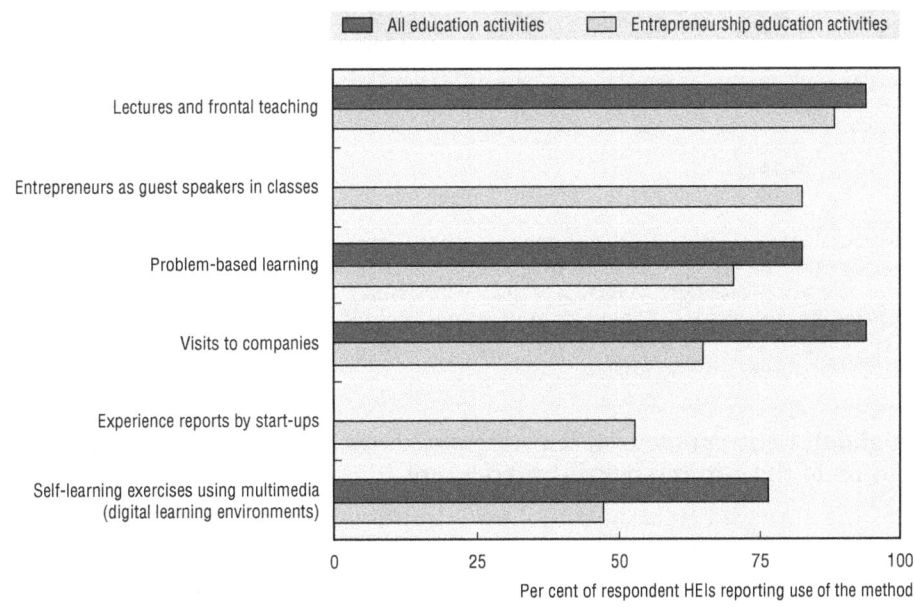

Notes: Higher education institutions (HEIs) were asked: "To what extent are the following teaching methods used at your HEI?" and "To what extent are the following teaching methods used in the entrepreneurship education activities currently offered at your HEI?". Response options for both questions were "not used", "rarely used", "regularly used", "primarily used". Accumulated responses for "regularly used" and "primarily used" are shown. The total number of responses analysed for this question was 17 (7 universities and 10 institutes of technology). The overall survey response rate was 81%. The survey response rates per HEI type are the following: universities (100%), institutes of technology (71%).
Source: OECD HEI Leader Survey Ireland (2015).

to participate in student associations, which are well established in all Irish HEIs. The HEI Leader Survey shows that there has been a large increase in student demand for informal learning opportunities across nearly all surveyed HEIs. The HEIs have prepared the ground for this with a broad range of communication activities used to advertise extra-curricular education activities on entrepreneurship (Figure 2.9). Most common is the use of social networks, such as Facebook and Twitter, special events, and information on websites. Less used were mailing lists, newsletters, and regular events such as fairs and dedicated round table meetings.

Figure 2.9. **Advertising extra-curricular entrepreneurship activities in Irish higher education**

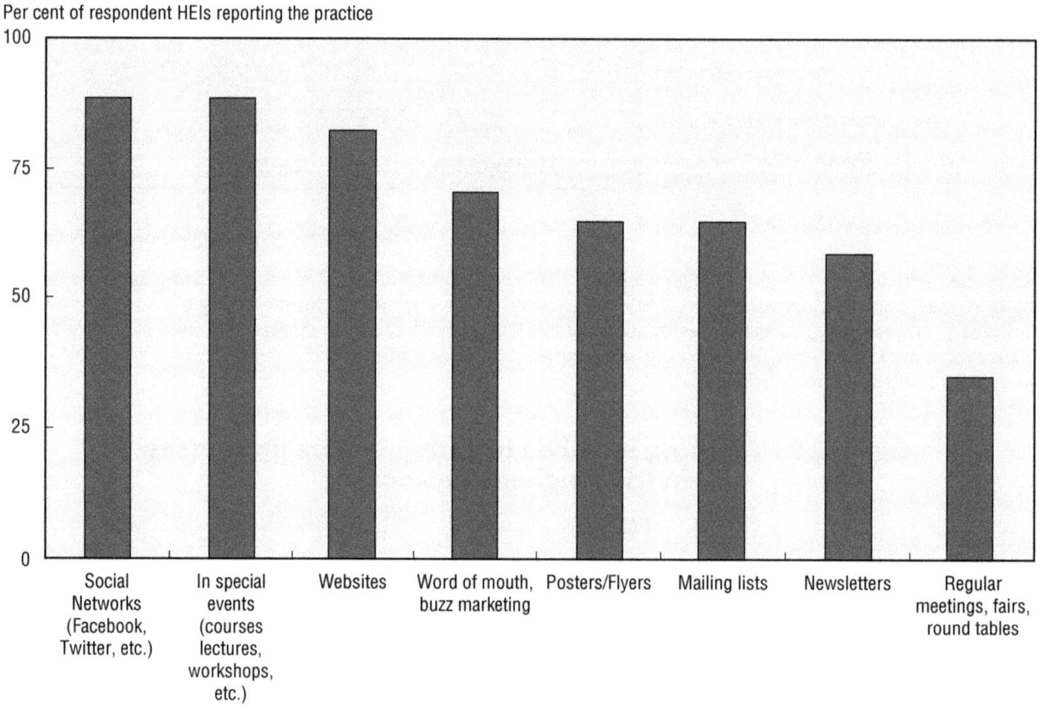

Per cent of respondent HEIs reporting the practice

[Bar chart showing approximate percentages: Social Networks (Facebook, Twitter, etc.) ~88%; In special events (courses lectures, workshops, etc.) ~88%; Websites ~82%; Word of mouth, buzz marketing ~70%; Posters/Flyers ~65%; Mailing lists ~65%; Newsletters ~58%; Regular meetings, fairs, round tables ~33%]

Notes: Higher education institutions (HEIs) that currently offer entrepreneurship education activities were asked: "How do you advertise the entrepreneurship education activities that are organised outside study curricula/programmes or open across faculties?". A total of 17 HEIs (7 universities, 10 institutes of technology) responded. The overall survey response rate was 81%. The survey response rates per HEI type are the following: universities (100%), institutes of technology (71%).
Source: OECD HEI Leader Survey Ireland (2015).

The HEI validates entrepreneurial learning outcomes which drives the design and execution of the entrepreneurial curriculum

60% of the surveyed HEIs, which offer entrepreneurship education activities, also undertake formal evaluations. When practiced this is mostly an obligatory procedure. The focus is on competence development and satisfaction of participants; half of the HEIs also measured the motivation of participants to start a business. In the majority of HEIs (83.3%) a specifically tailored survey instrument was used; and more than 40% reported that entrepreneurship education activities were also evaluated with focus groups. When a questionnaire was used it was mostly at the end of the course (75%); only two HEIs reported collecting data at multiple times in order to analyse the effectiveness of the course.

The HEI co-designs and delivers the curriculum with external stakeholders

Contact with external stakeholders in Irish HEIs occurs at all levels and across all units and is primarily focused on improving the relevance and impact of their teaching and learning, R&D and engagement strategies. The HEIs also avail of the expertise of external stakeholders on a regular short term, part-time and occasional basis to support entrepreneurial activities. Examples of this include the use of industry experts in course development and validation activities by all IOTs in the country, the use of external entrepreneurs as student mentors by the careers department, and the availability of entrepreneurs in residence within business school structures.

Figure 2.10 shows the extent to which the various stakeholders in higher education are engaged in entrepreneurship education activities. The results, which come from the HEI Leader Survey show that both the design and delivery of such activities is extensively shared with external stakeholders. Key partners are SMEs, individual entrepreneurs, technology parks and incubators, business support organisations, chambers of commerce as well as large firms. Also other HEIs are key partners in the design and delivery of these activities. Less frequent partners are business consultants, tax advisors and lawyers, venture capital providers, business angels and banks. Their involvement is more evident in the delivery of education activities than in the design phase. This kind of collaboration pattern also applies to multinational corporations.

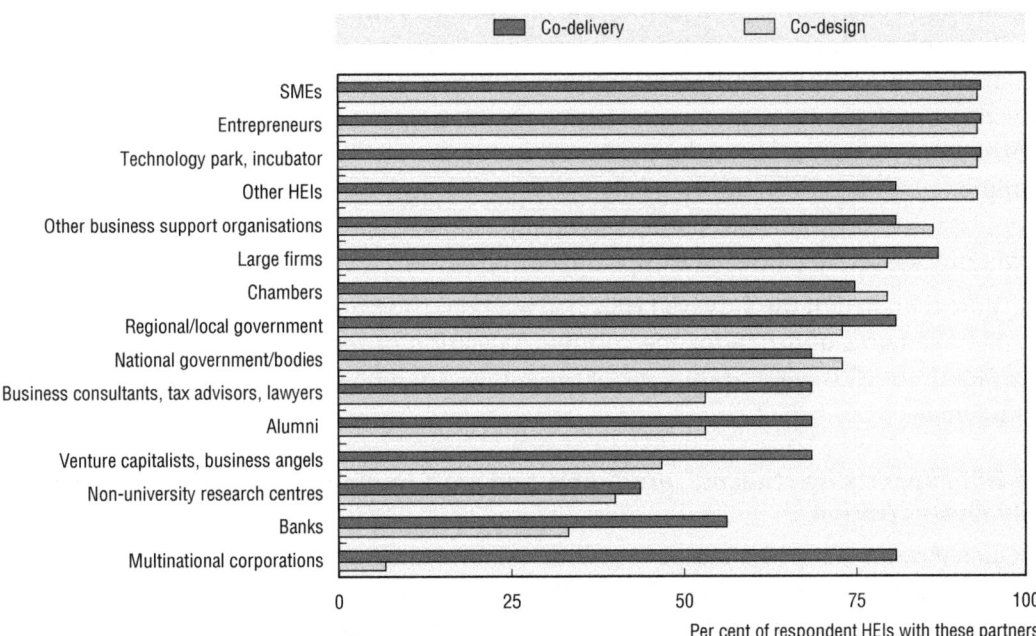

Figure 2.10. **Partners of Irish higher education institutions for entrepreneurship education**

Notes: Higher education institutions (HEIs) that currently offer entrepreneurship education activities were asked: "With which of the following organisations or individuals does your HEI collaborate regularly in the conceptual development of the entrepreneurship education activities?", "With which of the following organisations or individuals does your HEI maintain regular collaboration with in the delivery of the entrepreneurship education activities?". A total of 17 higher education institutions (7 universities, 10 institutes of technology) responded to these questions. The overall survey response rate was 81%. The survey response rates per HEI type are the following: universities (100%), institutes of technology (71%).
Source: OECD HEI Leader Survey Ireland (2015).

Results of entrepreneurship research are integrated into the entrepreneurial education offer

There are several well-connected networks of entrepreneurship educators and practitioners in Ireland (see Chapter 1). This greatly facilitates the inclusion of the results of entrepreneurship research in entrepreneurship teaching and course content.

Preparing and supporting entrepreneurs

The HEI increases awareness of the value of entrepreneurship and stimulates the entrepreneurial intentions of students, graduates and staff to start up a business or venture

The Irish higher education system as a whole actively encourages individuals to become more entrepreneurial through a wide, rich and innovative range of initiatives and programmes. These include undergraduate and postgraduate programme modules, work based learning initiatives, business start-up and business incubation programmes, mentoring initiatives and start-up funding for researchers (see Chapter 1).

Some HEIs expose students to entrepreneurship skills development at the latter stage of their undergraduate studies and expand on this during the course of taught postgraduate programmes. The approach across disciplines also varies, with entrepreneurship obviously appearing as a central theme within business programmes, but with a more limited presence within the Science, Technology and Engineering fields.

Business start-up programmes are available in all of the HEIs visited and are available to both students and staff as well as individuals outside of the higher education community. The Enterprise Ireland (EI) funded New Frontiers Entrepreneur Development Programme which runs in IOTs is regarded as a highly successful platform to provide support for individuals and groups to move entrepreneurial ideas into action (see Chapter 1 for more information). Communication is a priority and it is easy to find information about the entrepreneurial activities on the HEI's websites; on average it takes three "clicks" to get up-to-date information about entrepreneurship courses, hackathons, incubation facilities, co-working spaces, and other start-up support measures.

More than half of the surveyed HEIs had adopted rules and regulations concerning the use of trademarks and 70% for the commercialisation of research results. Slightly more than 60% of the HEIs were, at the time of the survey, shareholders in firms founded by staff or students.

The HEI supports its students, graduates and staff to move from idea generation to business creation

Irish government policy has put significant efforts into building a strong and sustainable entrepreneurship ecosystem (see Chapter 1), whose key pillars are i) culture, human capital and education, ii) business environment and support, iii) access to finance, iv) entrepreneurial networks and mentoring, v) access to markets, iv) innovation. The role of HEIs in this is only implicitly understood, however a clear definition of what the responsibilities and resources of HEIs are in each pillar will enhance the effectiveness of the system.

All of the visited HEIs provide extensive supports and facilities to assist individuals and groups in the business start-up and business support arenas. Supports provided include the use of on-site incubation space, mentoring by academic and business support staff, and use of specialised and advanced research and development facilities. In some instances, these services are provided on a pro bono basis but in general they are funded by external income sources such as the Enterprise Ireland innovation vouchers scheme.

Comparing the current offer of entrepreneurship education activities with the start-up support measures, there appears to be a gap for students in terms of start-up support. While students are the number one target for entrepreneurship education activities in both universities and IOTs, start-up support is more oriented towards researchers, professors, other staff members, alumni and people from outside the HEI (Figure 2.11). This gap is less obvious in IOTs.

Figure 2.11. **Target groups for entrepreneurship support in Irish higher education institutions**

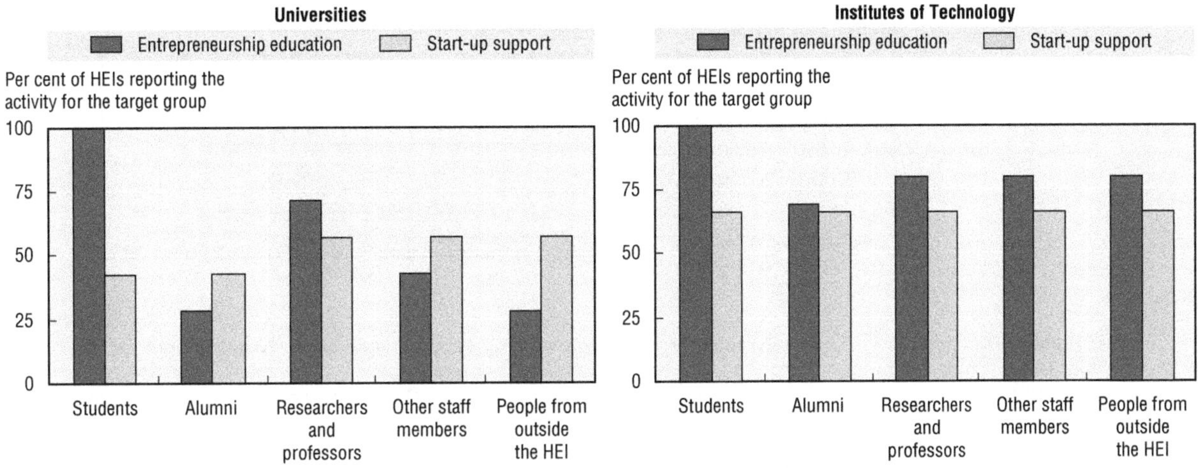

Notes: Higher education institutions (HEIs) that currently offer entrepreneurship education activities were asked: "Which of the following are target groups for the entrepreneurship education activities?" A total of 17 higher education institutions (7 universities, 10 institutes of technology) responded to the question. HEIs that currently offer start-up support were asked "Which of the following are target groups for the start-up support measures offered at your HEI?". A total of 16 HEIs (7 universities and 9 institutes of technology) responded to this question. The overall survey response rate was 81%. The survey response rates per HEI type are the following: universities (100%), institutes of technology (71%).
Source: OECD HEI Leader Survey Ireland (2015).

Interviews during the study visits confirmed that from a student perspective the use of real life projects and work placement opportunities exposed them to environments in which they encountered challenges that encouraged the development of their entrepreneurial skills. For those requiring support with business development ideas, entrepreneurship experience was more commonly gained through one-to-one or group mentoring activities provided by in house expertise, as well as external entrepreneurs in residence and links with supports available from other relevant external agencies.

All of the surveyed HEIs offer a wide range of start-up support measures (Figure 2.12). All provide assistance with handling intellectual property rights, preparation of business plans, support the application for public funding, refer nascent entrepreneurs and teams to external business support organisations, and offer access to infrastructure, such as incubation facilities and co-working spaces. Only one-third of the HEIs reported also providing financial resources. Nearly all HEIs noted an increased demand for assistance with applications for public funding and close to 70% reported an increased interest from nascent entrepreneurs in the HEI facilitating contacts with potential investors, such as venture capitalists, business angels and banks. Gaps between supply and demand are notable in relation to assistance with internationalisation and the provision of financial resources by the HEI itself.

Figure 2.12. **Offer and demand for start-up support measures**

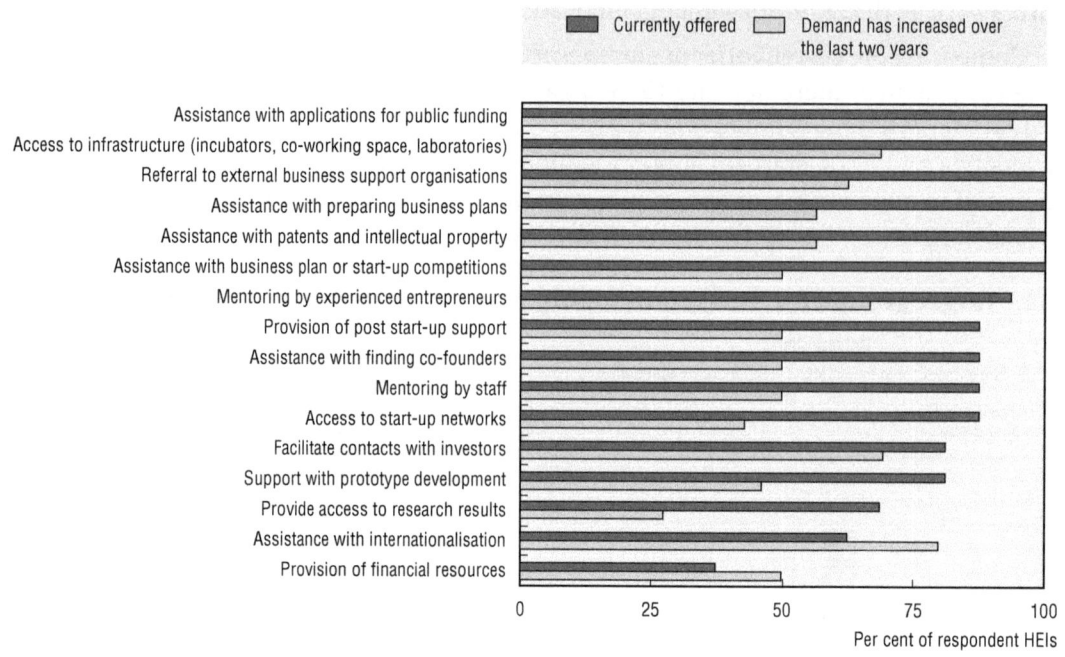

Notes: Higher education institutions (HEIs) that currently offer start-up support were asked: "You've stated earlier that your HEI currently offers special support measures for individuals or teams, who are interested in starting-up a business. What special support measures are currently offered?", "How has the demand for the special support measures developed over the last two years?". A total of 16 HEIs (7 universities and 9 institutes of technology) responded to this question. The overall survey response rate was 81%. The survey response rates per HEI type are the following: universities (100%), institutes of technology (71%).
Source: OECD HEI Leader Survey Ireland (2015).

Training is offered to assist students, graduates and staff in starting, running and growing a business

Start-up training courses, offered as part of the entrepreneurship education activities, provide relevant knowledge about financing, legal and regulatory issues, and human resource management. Soft skills, which are very important to effectively marshal resources and handle the start-up process are often acquired through out-of-class activities. HEIs in Ireland offer training to assist students, graduates and staff in starting, running and growing a business as part of the entrepreneurship education activities and through the incubation facilities.

The HEI Leader Survey shows the most practiced training methods in education activities are case studies, business idea generation activities, business plan writing and simulations or direct applications of how to start-up a business, or to further develop an entrepreneurial initiative (Figure 2.13). Less practiced but still common to more than half of the surveyed HEIs are, prototype development, case studies on companies in the region, exercises using the Business Model Canvas methodology, and case studies on company failure. Least practiced were simulations or direct applications of how to internationalise an entrepreneurial initiative.

Mentoring and other forms of personal development are offered by experienced individuals from academia or industry

Almost all HEIs reported that they offered mentoring by experienced entrepreneurs and slightly less offered mentoring by staff (Figure 2.12, above). Demand for mentoring has

Figure 2.13. **Start-up training offer in Irish higher education institutions**

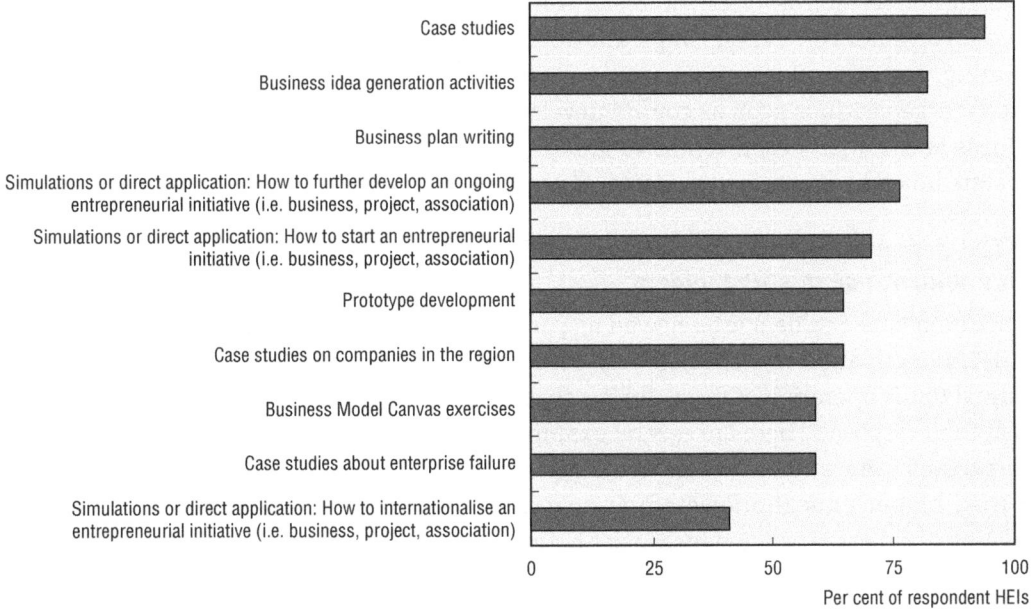

Notes: Higher education institutions (HEIs) that currently offer entrepreneurship education activities were asked: "To what extent are the following teaching methods currently used in the entrepreneurship education activities at your HEI?" A total of 17 higher education institutions (7 universities, 10 institutes of technology) responded to the question. Accumulated responses for "regularly used" and "primarily used" are shown. The overall survey response rate was 81%. The survey response rates per HEI type are the following: universities (100%), institutes of technology (71%).
Source: OECD HEI Leader Survey Ireland (2015).

increased over the last two years. More than 60% of the surveyed HEIs reported that mentoring nascent entrepreneurs was recognised along with other outstanding achievements in areas other than research and teaching.

The HEI facilitates access to financing for its entrepreneurs

The HEIs reported that they offered a range of measures to facilitate access to finance (Figure 2.12, above). All provided assistance with applications for public funding, more than 80% facilitate contacts with potential investors, such as venture capitalists and business angels and banks, and one-third of the HEIs provide financial resources.

The HEI offers or facilitates access to business incubation

All surveyed HEIs offer business incubation facilities on campus or support access to incubation facilities elsewhere. All of the on-campus incubation facilities offered coaching and training, access to the HEI's laboratories and use of the HEI's IT services. More than two-thirds of the surveyed HEIs also offer help with internationalisation and facilitate access to financing as part of their incubation facilities.

Knowledge exchange and collaboration

The HEI is committed to collaboration and knowledge exchange with industry, the public sector and society

As part of its National Strategy for Higher Education, Ireland has prioritised HEI engagement with society as one of three key mission pillars. Indeed, HEIs, through recent government policies and initiatives such as the Action Plan for Jobs and the Regional Skills

Fora, are being placed at the forefront and seen as key drivers of regional and national economic and societal development plans (see Chapter 1). All of the HEIs visited demonstrated active involvement in partnerships and relationships with a wide range of stakeholders including, for example, active participation and involvement with local, regional and national organisations such as county development boards, local and regional authorities, business and industry representative groups, chambers of commerce, professional bodies and state boards.

The HEI demonstrates active involvement in partnerships and relationships with a wide range of stakeholders

External stakeholders interviewed as part of the review process all expressed the view that HEI participation in networks and partnerships was not only of great value but also essential to the operation of these groups given the strength and range of expertise the HEIs had at their disposal. There are several examples of how researchers in HEIs helped firms to scale up their innovation activities (see Chapter 5). Indeed the success of R&D centres within the Irish higher education system is now more than ever based on the quality of the networks and partnerships which exist between the HEI and local, regional and national businesses and industry.

The HEIs visited presented ample evidence that they avail of every opportunity to link research, education and industry activities together to affect the whole knowledge ecosystem. This finding is confirmed by the results of the HEI Leader Survey which show the range of knowledge exchange practices and partners of HEIs (Figure 2.14). With regard to *ad hoc* or systematic involvement of external stakeholders in teaching, most common were partnerships with large firms, multinational corporations and SMEs. Similar patterns can be observed for the organisation of internships and different forms of technology and knowledge transfer. Temporary mobility schemes of academic staff (i.e. secondments) are organised mainly with large firms. Lifelong learning programmes are organised for, and with, a variety of organisations. Key partners for joint research initiatives and contract research include SMEs, large companies, multinational corporations, as well as other HEIs.

The geographic radius of knowledge exchange partners is large for the surveyed HEIs and included local contacts, as well as relationships with organisations located elsewhere in Ireland and within and outside the EU (Figure 2.15). Contacts with public/private research centres are mainly national, however 60% of the surveyed HEIs reported to have contacts within the wider EU area and 30% beyond. Relationships with other HEIs occur at all levels of geographic distance and they account for half of the HEIs' links with partners outside the EU. Collaboration with regional/local governments is focused on the close proximity to the HEI and 40% of the respondents collaborate with these organisations also elsewhere in the country. Relationships with SMEs are either local or national and for close to one-quarter also cover the wider EU area. Partners from large firms and multinational corporations are mostly located elsewhere in Ireland, however two-thirds of the HEIs also have local collaborations. Contacts with Chambers are mainly local. Relationships with Alumni are mainly within Ireland but also have global scope.

The HEI has strong links with incubators, science parks and other external initiatives

All surveyed HEIs offer business incubation on campus or facilitate access to incubation facilities elsewhere and most of the HEIs collaborate with technology parks and incubators for the design and delivery of entrepreneurship support activities (Figure 2.10,

Figure 2.14. **Partners of Irish higher education institutions in knowledge exchange activities**

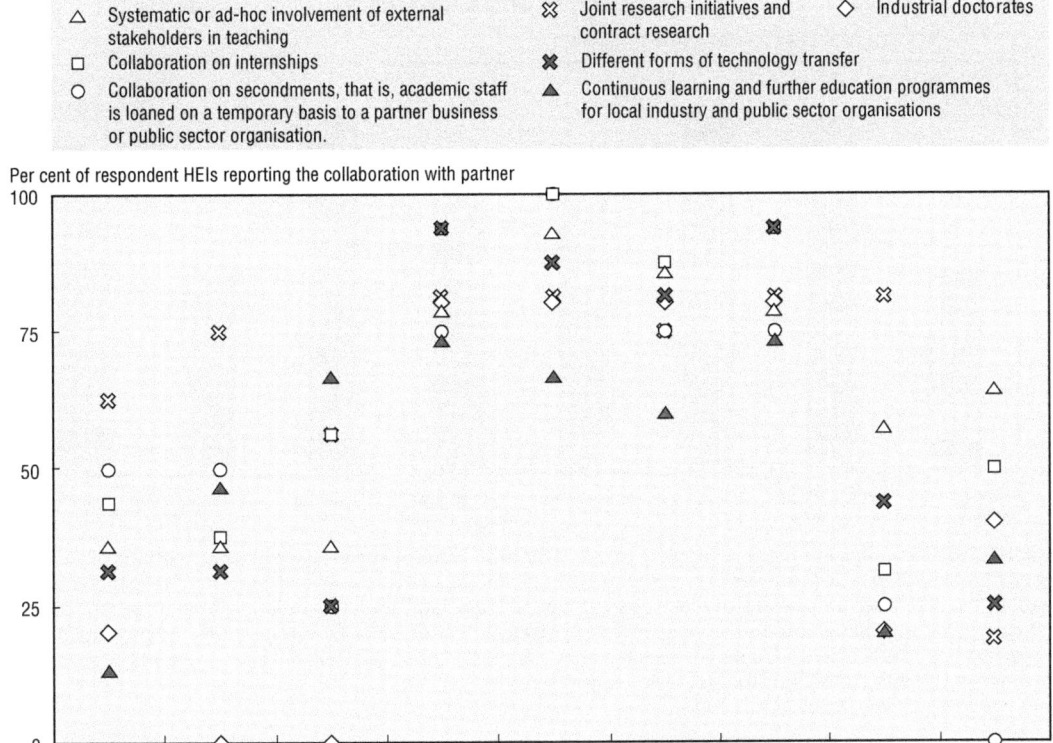

Notes: Higher education institutions (HEIs) were asked: "Knowledge exchange can take on various forms. The focus can be on teaching, research or any form of strategic collaboration. Which of the following are currently practiced at your HEI?"; "Which of the following are currently knowledge exchange partners of your HEI?". A total of 17 HEIs responded (7 universities, 10 institutes of technology). The following proportions of HEIs reported having knowledge exchange relationships of any kind: with public/private research centres – 59%, national government – 76%, regional/local government – 82%, SMEs – 94%, large firms –94%, multi-national corporations – 88%, Chambers – 53%, other HEIs – 88%, alumni – 59%. The overall survey response rate was 81%. The survey response rates per HEI type are the following: universities (100%), institutes of technology (71%).
Source: OECD HEI Leader Survey Ireland (2015).

above). In almost 70% of the HEIs the demand for incubation facilities increased over the last five years. Four HEIs reported having a representative of a technology park as a member of the HEI's governing body.

The HEI provides opportunities for staff and students to take part in innovative activities with business and the external environment

Opportunities exist to support staff and student mobility between academia and the external environment. However, in the case of staff mobility this is limited due to lack of funding and limitations surrounding terms and conditions of employment.

Internships are a common practice to offer students the opportunity to participate in innovative activities with business and the external environment. More than two-thirds of the HEIs offer internships for their students; 40% have mandatory internships across most of their programmes at Bachelor level, 50% at Masters level, and 35% for doctoral study programmes. Supports for students include, in order of current practice: access to

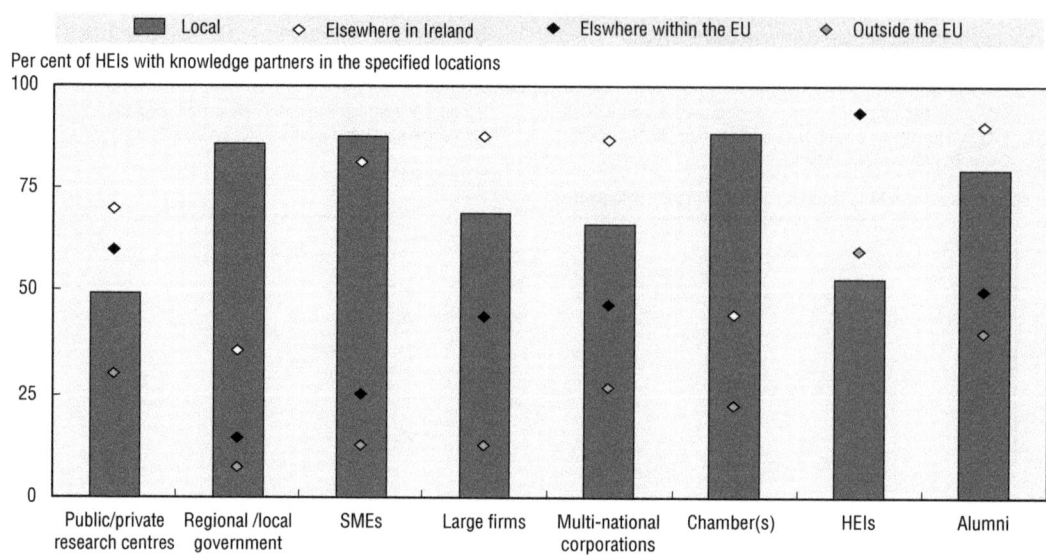

Figure 2.15. **Location of knowledge exchange partners of Irish higher education institutions**

Notes: Higher education institutions (HEIs) were asked: "Where are current knowledge exchange partners of your HEI located?". A total of 20 HEIs (7 universities, 10 institutes of technology and 3 colleges of education) responded to this question. The following proportions of HEIs reported having knowledge exchange relationships of any kind: with local partners – 94%, elsewhere in the country – 94%, elsewhere within the European Union – 94%, outside the European Union – 59%. The overall survey response rate was 81%. The survey response rates per HEI type are the following: universities (100%), institutes of technology (71%).
Source: OECD HEI Leader Survey Ireland (2015).

information about internship opportunities (86.7%), continuous support during mobility (86.7%), incentives for students to share their experiences with other students afterwards (40%), and financial support (33.3%).

Fewer initiatives exist to support the temporary mobility of HEI staff into industry and public organisations. Current practice was reported by only seven HEIs (35%) and a further four HEIs indicated that the introduction of secondment schemes is being considered by their governing authorities. The supports offered, in order of current practice, are: information about mobility opportunities (100%), continuous support during mobility (100%), incentives for staff to share their experiences after mobility (71%), and funding (57.1%).

The HEI integrates research, education and industry (wider community) activities to exploit new knowledge

There are several examples of projects where HEIs bring together research, education and the business community. They will be discussed in Chapters 3 and 5.

The internationalised institution

Internationalisation is an integral part of the HEI's entrepreneurial agenda

The international strategies of HEIs in all areas including student recruitment, exchange and placement activities; research and development, and staff mobility and recruitment are firmly rooted and have evolved from their active participation in international networks. Historically these networks commenced from participation in European projects but over time Irish HEIs have significantly expanded their internationalisation strategies and networks into the USA, Canada, Brazil, China, Malaysia and numerous countries in the Middle East. The

HEI Leader Survey confirms this. More than 40% of the HEIs have knowledge exchange partners from across the European Union and more than 20% have global relationships (Figure 2.15, above).

All HEIs visited presented strong and ambitious international strategies of an entrepreneurial nature which are largely focused on income generation from international student recruitment and participation in international education and R&D initiatives. Although the internationalisation strategies of universities were well established and advanced, the scale and ambition of internationalisation in the IOTs was also impressive in terms of participation in international research projects, internships abroad and initiatives to facilitate international staff mobility.

The HEI explicitly supports the international mobility of its staff and students.

Common internationalisation practices of Irish HEIs include collaboration within Erasmus+, which is part of the European Region Action Scheme for the Mobility of University Students, international student exchange programmes and student internships abroad, international research collaboration, and joint international education programmes (e.g. double degree programmes). One university and one institute of technology reported that they had overseas campuses (Figure 2.16). Universities are slightly more active in these internationalisation activities than the IOTs.

Figure 2.16. **Internationalisation activities of Irish higher education institutions**

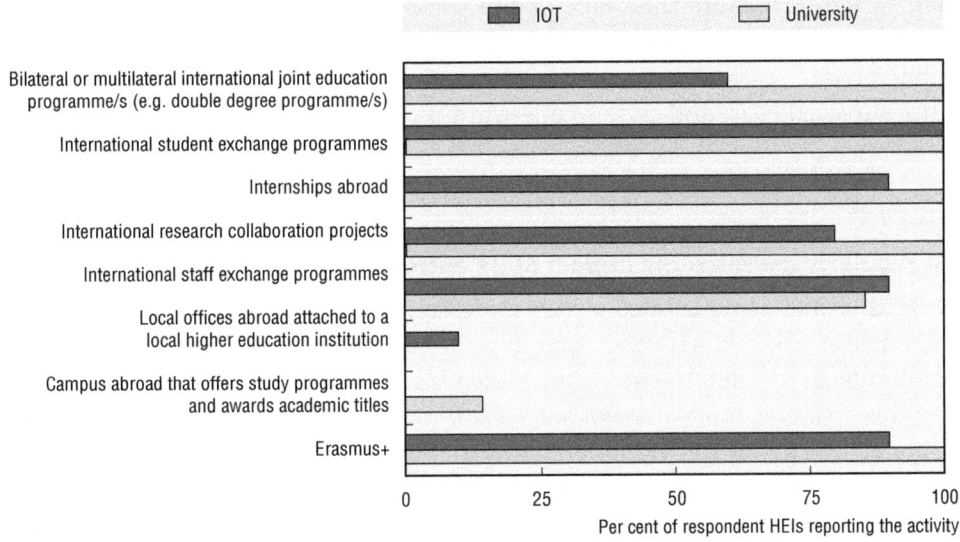

Notes: Higher education institutions (HEIs) were asked to report on their current internationalisation activities. A total of 17 higher education institutions (7 universities, 10 institutes of technology) responded to the question. The overall survey response rate was 81%. The survey response rates per HEI type are the following: universities (100%), institutes of technology (71%).
Source: OECD HEI Leader Survey Ireland (2015).

Outward staff mobility programmes in Ireland are, in the main, funded by external sources. The recent economic situation has impacted negatively on outward staff mobility programmes with fewer opportunities being made available. In contrast, HEIs referenced and demonstrated significant success in recruiting staff and, in particular, research staff from abroad through a number of initiatives, including collaborations with other like-minded international partners.

Inward student mobility in the main is driven by progressive recruitment campaigns which project Ireland as English speaking and as being a country with an open and welcoming environment within the European Union. Fees for international students who choose to come to Ireland are also considered to be quite competitive in comparison to other international jurisdictions. Outward student mobility numbers in Ireland are principally driven by Erasmus programmes. A number of HEIs reference the American J1 visa programme as being one of the most successful outward student mobility programmes for Irish students. This, however, is a student working visa programme as opposed to an educational exchange programme. Inward student mobility significantly outnumbers outward student mobility. This was mentioned by all of the visited HEIs as a significant issue of concern.

The HEI seeks and attracts international and entrepreneurial staff

Irish HEIs are attractive employers for researchers and academic staff members from abroad. 70% of the surveyed HEIs reported to have recruitment policies and practices that seek to attract international staff. This was slightly more common (76.9%) for entrepreneurship education activities. More than half of the HEIs were recruiting international staff for their start-up support measures.

The international dimension is reflected in the HEI's approach to research

Many HEIs are part of various international research networks with reach beyond the European Union (EU). More than 80% of the surveyed HEIs have knowledge exchange relationships with HEIs in the wider EU area, and 50% also with HEIs globally. Collaboration with public/private research organisations located elsewhere in the EU was practiced by 60% of the surveyed HEIs, and close to one-third collaborated with research organisations globally.

Measuring impact

The HEI regularly assesses the impact of its entrepreneurial agenda

The HEIs visited demonstrated a wide understanding of impact in terms of education, research, engagement and networks, and in terms of academic and non-academic results inside and outside the HEI. Impact is generated through non-linear processes, which are multi-iterative, parallel, multi-dimensional, absorptive and combine push and pull factors. Impact is not just about individual endeavours but systemic, taking into account how individual actions related to past, current and future activities at departmental, faculty and institutional levels. Generation and diffusion of impact needs supportive and flexible structures, communication infrastructure and skilled people. Communication is particularly important as impact related information is both qualitative and quantitative, it can be fuzzy in its nature and it is spread over time and different sources.

Ireland has introduced a sector-wide performance management system for its HEIs. As part of this process each HEI agrees an individual compact with the Higher Education Authority (HEA) on an annual basis and a portion of each HEI's state grant is awarded based on performance relative to targets set in the compact. The HEA monitors a wide range of HEI-specific, as well as common metrics on an annual basis including enrolments by programme type and discipline, graduate statistics and research outcomes including research income, spin-offs and patents (see Chapter 1 for more information). Self-assessment is a key component of the performance management process. The use of the HEInnovate tool by

Irish HEIs can therefore be a useful ongoing practice. It will be important that HEIs are supported in self-reflection practices, in particular, in terms of exchanging information and learning from each other. Individual HEIs or groups of HEIs within Ireland should consider creating strong collaborative and/or mentor links with other HEIs from the HEInnovate network at home and abroad that are advancing and embedding entrepreneurship and innovation within their strategies and practices.

As it stands the performance evaluation system does not fully evaluate the economic or social impact of supporting entrepreneurship and innovation in higher education. Individual HEIs, however, have introduced various impact measurements in this area. The HEI Leader Survey shows that 70% of the HEIs had introduced performance indicators for their entrepreneurial agenda (Figure 2.1, above).

The HEI regularly assesses how its personnel and resources support its entrepreneurial agenda

There are significant opportunities to impact on the local/regional economy, not only directly but in a wide range of indirect ways, both on the supply and demand side. If Irish businesses do not have the capacity to absorb the research, knowledge and skills coming out of HEIs then the danger is that these "leak" out of the region or country to other places with higher innovation capacity, creating an "innovation paradox" whereby high innovating places benefit from the investment made in lower innovating places, reinforcing the hierarchy of regions and countries as the strong places become ever stronger. This will be discussed in Chapter 4.

The HEI regularly assesses entrepreneurial teaching and learning across the institution

Assessing the impact of education activities is usually conducted by individual departments/units and for individual activities. Work placement programmes in all visited HEIs provided evidence of improved student performance on return from their placement period. Evaluation is also common practice for entrepreneurship education activities. 80% of the surveyed IOTs and 57% of the universities reported to have formal procedures established for this. Quality and Qualifications Ireland (QQI) has issued guidelines on quality assurance to HEIs following the principle of providing HEIs with ownership of the guidelines.

The HEI regularly assesses the impact of start-up support

Close to 70% of the surveyed HEIs that currently provide start-up support measures evaluate their impact. This is slightly lower than evaluation of entrepreneurship education activities. All of the HEIs visited carry out regular monitoring and evaluation of their knowledge exchange activities and start-up support activities. The level of monitoring and evaluation in all instances was comprehensive and included measurement of the number of start-ups, spin-offs, patents, new research ideas and research relationships. This included participant satisfaction with available programmes, the monitoring of levels of job creation and income produced by start-up support measures. The level of monitoring and range of measures was relatively consistent across the HEIs and appeared, in the main, to be based on funding agency requirements as part of their reporting and evaluation processes.

The HEI regularly assesses knowledge exchange and collaboration

Irish HEIs are active in a range of knowledge exchange activities. There are many examples of innovative and impactful research taking place in Irish HEIs. However, it might be fair to say that individual HEIs, research groups, and the sector as a whole, have not been effective at telling their story and making the case for funding and investment. While there are numerous sources of information on various activities, these are not being translated effectively enough into details of their actual impacts in terms of the economy and society as a whole.

The HEI Leader Survey gathered information on certain activities and whether evaluation practices are in place. Most HEIs reported having formal evaluation practices in place for their technology transfer activities; also most of the pilot initiatives on industrial doctorates, the lifelong learning activities and collaboration on staff secondment are evaluated by the HEIs. Gaps can be noted for the evaluation of collaboration on internships, the systematic involvement of external stakeholders in teaching and joint research initiatives (Figure 2.17).

Figure 2.17. **Evaluation practice of knowledge exchange activities in Irish higher education**

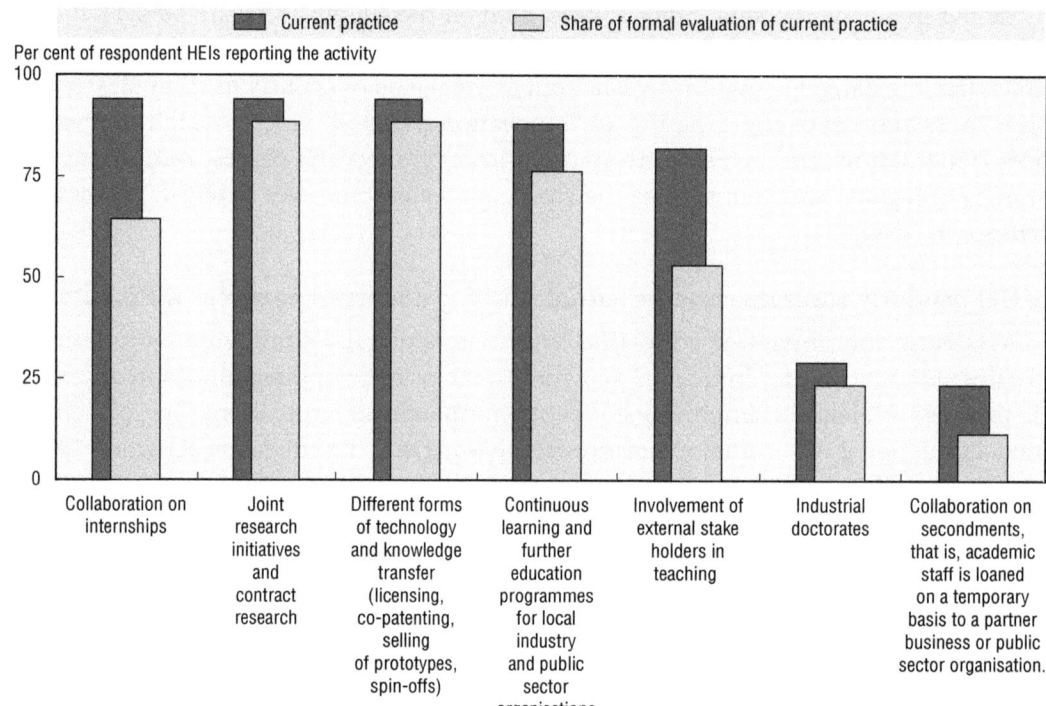

Notes: Higher education institutions (HEIs) were asked: "Knowledge exchange can take on various forms. The focus can be on teaching, research or any form of strategic collaboration. Which of the following are currently practiced at your HEI?". For each of the reported knowledge exchange practice the HEIs were asked "Is there a formal evaluation practice of these knowledge exchange activities?". Percentage shares of formal evaluation of a specific knowledge exchange practice are shown. A total of 17 HEIs (7 universities and 10 institutes of technology) responded to this question. The overall survey response rate was 81%. The survey response rates per HEI type are the following: universities (100%), institutes of technology (71%).
Source: OECD HEI Leader Survey Ireland (2015).

The HEI regularly assesses its international activities in relation to its entrepreneurial agenda

The HEIs visited all track their international activities in considerable detail. However, there is room to undertake more sophisticated impact assessments to understand where further investments would have the greatest effect (see Chapter 5).

Recommendations for public policy action

Enhance collaboration between policy structures and state agencies involved in supporting entrepreneurship and innovation in HEIs

As part of the development of the National Policy Statement on Entrepreneurship significant efforts were put into building a strong and sustainable entrepreneurship ecosystem. The role of HEIs in this is only implicitly understood, however. A clear definition of what the responsibilities and resources of HEIs are in each pillar will enhance the effectiveness of the system. Co-ordination and communication with the help of existing cross-departmental and cross-agency higher education structures should be continually improved regarding programme activity and policy development. It will be important to consider approaches which may result in a consolidation of national funding programmes under a high-level co-ordination committee where research funders would meet to discuss policy objectives, future planning etc. on a regular basis.

Regional collaborative initiatives involving HEIs, such as the Regional Clusters and the Regional Skills Fora, are not only the building blocks of the 21st century Higher Education System in Ireland, but the initial stage for the development of knowledge and innovation regions in Ireland. As such it is timely to devote renewed attention to the initiative. To achieve the overall aim of these initiatives requires strengthening research capacity and capability, promoting enterprise and innovation, and attracting and retaining talent from home and abroad. A future phase in regional initiatives needs to focus on knowledge producers, users and transformers from businesses, industry and civil society. Sharing good practices amongst the regional initiatives through a "learning from each other" platform involving the governing bodies of the different regional groupings will be important. Coupled with this, HEIs and other stakeholders should be encouraged to come forward with specific development initiatives in order to avoid the process becoming too "top-down".

Broaden the scope for inter- and transdisciplinary research initiatives in research priorities, and in the effort to mobilise HEIs in local and regional development

Addressing societal challenges increasingly requires interdisciplinary collaboration between medical, technological and scientific research interwoven with research questions and practices from the arts, humanities and social sciences. Conceptualising the research process and the impact of research only through the lenses of commercialisation and market opportunities will set too narrow a focus. Broadening the awareness and understanding of researchers of the (potential) impact of their research can counteract this. HEIs and research funders could explore the use of innovative tools to bring together researchers from different disciplines in order to build collaborative projects and proposals. Inter- and transdisciplinary research can also be crucial in mobilising HEIs for local development.

Review current employment control restrictions in higher education to allow for enhanced engagement activities with business and society

Revisions in terms and conditions of employment in higher education should be considered to allow for enhanced structured engagement with external stakeholders including the provision of industry sabbaticals/exchange and recognition of academic/industry consultancy activities. To support, encourage and implement even short two to three week staff mobility initiatives on a sector wide scale would greatly enhance the entrepreneurial culture across the higher education system.

Continue targeted state investment in internationalisation initiatives

The Irish higher education system would benefit greatly from continued targeted state investment in internationalisation initiatives rather than remaining largely dependent on external funding sources to cover the costs of international programmes. The review of the working visa system for international graduates which is being undertaken is most welcome. The time allowed to recently qualified international students to stay and work in Ireland after completing their studies should be increased.

Support HEIs in Ireland in creating collaborative and mentor links with entrepreneurial HEIs abroad

Individual HEIs or groups of HEIs within Ireland should consider creating strong collaborative and/or mentor links with HEIs abroad, who are advancing and embedding entrepreneurship and innovation within their strategies and practices. There is a role for public policy in facilitating peer learning in a systemic approach rather than single HEIs building their own links.

Introduce a system-wide exercise to document impact of entrepreneurship and innovation in higher education

There are many examples of innovative and impactful teaching and learning and research taking place in Irish HEIs. Information about these needs to be made widely available and such good practice should be replicated and promoted. A national exercise is recommended to document the impact of entrepreneurship and innovation in higher education. This would require a common approach involving all funders and the introduction of a common research classification system and, in as far as possible, an agreed dataset to be collected (with additional indicators where required for particular agencies). This would make it much easier to build a common interface and share data. Mechanisms should be put in place to provide researchers with more capacity in terms of time, resources and administrative support to seek and apply for research opportunities and funding, and document impact. In order to facilitate collaboration and engagement between higher education and enterprise – at the institutional and individual staff levels – review mechanisms and metrics are required to achieve parity of esteem across disciplines, types of activities, and to increase the understanding of impact.

Recommendations for higher education institutions

Expand entrepreneurship education across all disciplines and increase the number of interdisciplinary education activities

Further innovation in teaching and programme delivery should be encouraged, for example through more project-based learning, blended learning, placements and co-operative models. Entrepreneurship education and training could be offered to all students in more formalised and accredited ways. There is a risk that entrepreneurship education is perceived as a "factory producing start-ups", with an emphasis on functional dimensions and business planning. Efforts should be increased to organise education activities on creativity, innovation and entrepreneurship, which involve students from different faculties and departments in the form of (optional) interdisciplinary modules throughout the duration of their studies. The organisation of interdisciplinary idea generation workshops, which bring together researchers, students and knowledge users, can be a good starting point for more collaboration across disciplines. To engage staff, a specific award could be introduced for interdisciplinary achievements, such as the development and application of conceptualisations, theories, sources and methods that are drawn from different disciplines in order to define and resolve problems in novel ways.

Expand the number of places available on venture creation programmes, particularly for students and alumni

The expansion of the number of places available on business start-up programmes is recommended given the success of existing programmes and current demand for places, particularly among students. This expansion should also include increased investment in the physical infrastructure used to house new ventures. Opening venture creation programmes to alumni should be considered.

Incentivise and support staff engagement in knowledge exchange and collaboration

Increased prioritisation and investment in staff mobility programmes between academia and the external environment is required. Adjustment of staff contracts and terms and conditions of employment to promote and facilitate such programmes should also be considered. Incentives should be provided within HEIs to enhance enterprise engagement activities as part of the assessment process for promotion. Also, HEIs should increase the number of support staff who can help to spot opportunities and engineer the interdisciplinary and external partnerships.

Enhance collaboration with small and medium-sized enterprises through a single "front door"

Involving small and traditional firms in knowledge exchange activities requires a strategy that provides the partner firm with quick wins (e.g. updating the ICT capacity), as well as a portfolio of follow-up activities that are beneficial for both the firm and the HEI (or the partner academic). Work placements and co-operative learning arrangements, as well as the Regional Skills Fora, are good starting points. Both can help to build the relationships that lead to more transformational, long-term relationships between businesses and HEIs.

Notes

1. It is mandatory for Irish higher education institutions (HEIs) to have written and formally approved strategic plans. This was confirmed by the OECD HEI Leader Survey. All of the 20 surveyed HEIs reported that their institution had a strategic document that states its vision, mission and values. The survey also indicated that strategies are prepared with inputs from a wide range of relevant stakeholders.
2. See Chapters 1 and 4 for more information about lifelong learning programmes in Irish HEIs.

References

OECD (2015), HEI Leader Survey Ireland, implemented as part of the HEInnovate country review of Ireland.

Chapter 3

Enhancing the organisational capacity of Ireland's higher education institutions

> *This chapter expands on the findings presented in Chapter 2 related to enhancing organisational capacity. It examines organisational capacity from a system-level perspective and discusses the current restructuring of the higher education system, the steering mechanisms and funding of research in higher education institutions. The chapter discusses the further development of the Regional Clusters and the next generation of regional collaborative fora (e.g. Regional Skills Fora). The chapter also reviews current practices undertaken by higher education institutions to enhance and sustain their organisational capacity primarily with regard to research and knowledge exchange.*

Introduction

Entrepreneurship and innovation in higher education are no longer only associated with business start-ups and technology transfer. They are also referred to as procedural frameworks for how organisations and individuals behave, for example, in creating and nurturing links between teaching and research, organising societal engagement and knowledge exchange, and building and managing resources for effective partnerships. In short, being an entrepreneurial and innovative higher education institution (HEI) means to discover and act upon opportunities, which initially may appear to be challenges. In doing so, HEIs need to continuously augment their organisational capacity. A common starting point is the presence of an all-encompassing leadership, strategic planning and professional management framework. Adequate funding, a high level of institutional autonomy, accountability mechanisms that allow for flexibility and agility, as well as close links with strategic partners at local, national and international levels are indispensable building blocks.

Ireland has been hit hard by the economic crisis starting in 2008. It is now well on its way to recovery after an austerity programme which has very severely restricted investment in fundamental areas and resulted in unprecedented cuts in the public sector. The country has a favourable demographic situation. With a population of 4.6 million people and an average age of 34 years, Ireland has one of the youngest populations in Europe. It also has one of the highest rates of tertiary education attainment in the age group 30-34 years old (52.3% in 2015). The initiative of the Irish government to attract the Irish diaspora back to Ireland to live and work is important in augmenting the country's labour market.

Higher education in Ireland is one of the sectors which has experienced significantly large cuts. In the period 2008-14 public funding decreased by about 25%. Over the same period, the number of core staff in HEIs has been reduced by about 13% while student numbers have risen by 15%. Expenditure per student has declined by 24% from 2008 to 2016. Since 2014, there have been financial incentives and penalties implemented as part of the Strategic Dialogue process (see below), which are expected to reach up to 10% of total available funding.

Challenges facing policy makers and the higher education system in the coming years include: i) meeting the needs of a diverse student population, including school leavers and mature learners,[1] ii) building interdisciplinary research areas and links with teaching and learning in higher education, iii) widening participation while reflecting the changing composition and diversity of the population at all levels of education, iv) making the case for increased funding for higher education and research which competes with other high priority areas for public funding including health, social housing and primary and second-level education.

Generally speaking, the public budget for higher education may be distributed according to various models. In most European countries a formula is used to calculate the amount to be allocated to publicly funded HEIs. Through a set of indicators and their respective weights, the higher education system is steered to meet national priorities. The indicators, approximately 26 on average, include the number of students (input related indicator), the number of graduates (output), the graduate employment rate, community outreach etc. A model common in many countries is multi-annual contract funding, covering a period of two to three years, to enable better planning. This may also include measures to be taken in the event of unmet targets or if the state does not have enough means to provide the agreed amount of funding.[2]

In Ireland, public funding for higher education and research is distributed to HEIs through two mechanisms: i) a block grant which provides funding for core teaching and research activities and ii) competitive research awards. The block grant is a combined grant for core teaching and research activities and the Higher Education Authority (HEA) is responsible for distributing the funding amongst HEIs. Funds are allocated, primarily, using an input based formula which takes into account student numbers, weighted according to the area and level of the programme. Widening participation is incentivised through weighting more favourably students coming from non-traditional backgrounds. Research activity is incentivised by applying a higher weighting to research students. Furthermore, 5% of the core allocation to universities is top-sliced and allocated on the basis of research criteria – research degrees awarded and contract research income per academic staff. A stability mechanism of limiting budget variations to 2% in comparison with the previous year is in place. A review of the current funding model, known as the Recurrent Grant Allocation Model or RGAM, is currently underway.

Research funding in Irish higher education has decreased in recent years due to the economic crisis. This has arisen from both a reduction in targeted competitive research grants and also a reduction in core funding to higher education. There is no separate core funding stream for research, as is the case in some OECD countries, but the HEA block grant is clearly defined as a combined grant for supporting both teaching and research in HEIs. While the funding is allocated to HEIs using the formula described above, HEIs have full discretion in how this funding is used within their institution across the full range of disciplines and activities. In terms of research, this funding provides core support for research capacity including academic research salaries, support staff, overhead expenses, library services etc. This is complemented by competitive research funding programmes which are managed by a number of research funding agencies. These support specific projects and range from individual scholarships and fellowships to large research centres.

According to Eurostat data, state investment in research and development (R&D) in higher education in 2014 was estimated at 0.33% of gross domestic product (GDP), well below the provisional European Union average of 0.47%, and the provisional estimated 1.01% of GDP invested in Denmark, a suitable reference country for Ireland in terms of size. In the National Reform Programme, and Europe 2020 strategy a new target of gross domestic expenditure on R&D (GERD) of 2% of GDP is to be achieved by 2020 (1.52% in 2014). It is desirable that investment in R&D be increased to 3% of GDP as in other European countries.

R&D activities are essential for the long term growth of an economy. Disruptive innovations related to information and communications technology (ICT), such as Big Data, quantum computing and the Internet of Things are changing the ways in which we work and live. In the period 2010-12 inventions in these domains accounted for over two-thirds of patents filed in Europe and the United States. In this, R&D activities in higher education play an important role. Also relevant in this regard is raising the absorptive capacity for knowledge transfer through lifelong learning. According to latest available cross-country data, Ireland has the highest share of employment in the ICT sector and its sub-sectors at 5.14 % in 2013, compared to the OECD average of 2.85% (OECD, 2015).[3] ICT skills, particularly in small and medium-sized firms (SMEs), are crucial for firm survival and growth in the digital economy. An important policy objective is to seek to increase the level of ICT skills in the working population at all levels of education and training. Ireland has several excellent examples in this regard, such as the Springboard programme, addressed at reskilling and upskilling of the work force, and the ICT Skills Action Plan (see Chapter 1).

The European Commission has recently published the results of a foresight exercise on intelligent policy choices for Europe 2050 where it is proposed that a Europe of success will be characterised by "clusters of well-funded, internationally renowned universities thriving in strong partnerships with regional institutions" (EC, 2015). A case shall be made within the European Union for "Open Science" and all European regions will need to engage with this new reality. Areas for action include supporting infrastructure development, ensuring data access and literacy, reforming intellectual property rules, opening markets and programmes and enabling citizen participation. To achieve these aims expertise is needed (engineers, data management specialists, etc.) but also capital investment for computer networks, data repositories, archives and so on. Training people to work with data, and open access to data are fundamental building blocks. In this regard, regional collaborative initiatives in Ireland involving HEIs, as discussed in this chapter, are timely and promising.

Governance and steering of higher education, research and innovation in Ireland is shared between the Department of Education and Skills (DES) and the Department of Jobs, Enterprise and Innovation (DJEI). While DES has sole responsibility for governance and oversight of the higher education sector, the responsibility for R&D policy and funding is split between the two departments, with DJEI being the stronger partner in that respect. This is the result of a reorganisation of departmental responsibilities in 2010/11 when training came to DES and more elements of research went to DJEI. To avoid competing policies and overlapping funding instruments a high level of communication and shared decision making processes are of central importance. The cross-government governance and implementation structures, which are part of the Innovation 2020 strategy, the country's research and innovation strategy, are an important framework for achieving this.

Analysis and findings

Organisational capacity from a system-level perspective

Steering mechanisms in the Irish higher education system

To achieve better co-ordination of the higher education offer at regional and national levels, avoiding duplication and responding adequately to the demand, and at the same time guaranteeing institutional autonomy balanced with public accountability three steering mechanisms were introduced in the Irish higher education system. These are the system performance framework, the strategic dialogue leading to the institutional compacts, and the performance funding (See also Chapter 1). Also, the current review of the Recurrent Grant Allocation Model (RGAM) is expected to strengthen the steering of the system through general funding allocation.

The system performance framework is based on a strategic dialogue that was established between the HEA and each HEI and resulted in mission-based performance agreements, the so-called institutional compacts. The compact provides a strategic framework for the relationship between each HEI and the government: each compact aligns the mission and goals of the individual HEI with the national priorities for higher education. The compact also details funding commitments and objective indicators of success.

The compacts constitute a performance incentive framework, which enables the necessary steering of the higher education system while maintaining the autonomy of the HEIs and focusing on the need for accountability. As such, the approach is a model from which other higher education systems can learn. The most important learning points are:

- Dealing with duplication of academic offers and spurious competition amongst HEIs in a constructive way.
- Achieving a smooth transition pathway for students between institutions and programmes.
- Achieving a smooth transition between further education and higher education.
- Providing an offer at regional level that goes from short cycle certificates (further education) to PhD.
- Agreeing on quantitative success indicators and how achievement is rewarded.
- Respecting institutional autonomy and the need for accountability.

In 2014 an element of performance funding was introduced whereby financial incentives and penalties are being implemented as part of the compact review process, reaching up to 10% of total available funding. As it currently stands, this is a zero-sum-exercise since the money used for incentives comes from top-slicing the total amount which, at best, remains the same. The net result is an allocation model, which is based on prior performance instead of actual outputs.

Reconfiguration through mergers and regional initiatives

Higher education in Ireland is offered by public and private HEIs of three types: universities, institutes of technology (IOTs), and specialised colleges. In an attempt to overcome fragmentation, avoid duplication of programmes, give a better response to the needs of regional development and ensure sustainability, a major reconfiguration and rationalisation of the system has been recently initiated. The reform process is a major step towards transforming a collection of loosely bound HEIs into a system which is capable of dealing with the challenges of the 21st century.

Mergers of HEIs are part of this process. Typically, mergers are difficult and complex; and success is highly dependent on the quality of planning and implementation phases. Success factors identified from extant mergers include: creation of an inspiring vision for the new institution, identification of the expected gains, managing the staff allegiances, values and cultural differences and involving students. Moreover, the new HEI should recognise and respect the heritage and achievements of the formerly independent HEIs in a way that does not affect the creation and performance of the new HEI.

One strand of this development is the merger of small colleges of education into universities. The aim is to create larger and more dynamic institutions that are capable of accommodating diversity of views and backgrounds. The merger of St Patrick College Drumcondra, Mater Dei Institute of Education and the Church of Ireland College of Education with Dublin City University (DCU) is an example of this which illustrates some of the key challenges of mergers. There are significant cultural differences between the institutions, the smaller colleges are much older than DCU and have strong religious affiliations. The challenges in managing staff allegiances, values and cultural differences have been addressed through various work streams, a series of staff engagement workshops and other fora. This merger has been reported as a case study in a European project led by the European University Association (EUA, 2015).

Another proposed initiative is the merger of several IOTs with the possibility of providing the amalgamated HEI the status of a technological university. This process raises significant questions including the view, by international standards, that Ireland already has a high number of universities (although all of the existing universities would be classed as "traditional" universities and would have a different mission to technological universities).

A technological university will be distinguished by a mission and ethos that is aligned and consistent with the current mission and focus of institutes of technology with an emphasis on programmes at levels 6 to 8 and industry focused research. A technological university will also be expected to play a pivotal role in facilitating access and progression particularly through relationships with the further education and training sector. The proposed functions of a technological university include a strong focus on engagement with employers and regional development.

It will be important to ensure that a compelling vision for each of the proposed technological universities is created, that appropriate external stakeholder involvement is facilitated in mission development, and that appropriate resource models are developed and made available to ensure the process results in real value-added for the higher education system as a whole.

A further step in the development of the higher education system has been the Regional Clusters initiative, with the stated aim to facilitate extensive collaboration of HEIs and engagement with businesses, industry and civil society in order to build vibrant regional innovation systems. Six Regional Clusters were formed building on prior initiatives, such as the Atlantic University Alliance (AUA), created in 1999, and the Shannon Consortium formed in 2006 (see Box 3.1, below). The Regional Clusters initiative showed that a "one-size-fits-all approach" does not work. Each of the Regional Clusters had to adequately reflect the institutional, local and regional realities, taking into consideration previous experiences with the aim of enhancing synergies and co-ordination in education programmes and student pathways for the benefit of the region.

Within the regional initiatives, the fundamental objective is the creation of dynamic and innovative regions. Achieving this objective needs the co-ordinated engagement of knowledge users (and in some cases transformers) from business, industry and society. Of particular value is the presence of regional and national R&D players in regional initiatives. Their presence and commitment to regional initiatives, such as Regional Clusters and Regional Skills Fora, will be crucial for transforming regional groupings into vibrant knowledge hubs. Key to this is also the mobility of research staff between higher education and industry.

Regional clusters perform two integral and symbiotic roles – one is inward-looking and the other one is outward-facing. Good progress has been made with regard to the inward-looking role, particularly as far as collaboration of HEIs is concerned. However, more efforts are needed to build and strengthen the outward-facing role of the Regional Clusters and any future regional collaborative initiatives involving HEIs, such as the Regional Skills Fora. This situation is to be expected as HEIs tend to react in a conservative way to any process that presents and values them as elements of a larger system instead of unique independent institutions competing with each other for students and funding.

At the current stage of the Strategic Dialogue, institutional compacts have been agreed and signed. It is now important to press on with regional initiatives in order to join the dots in the education system. To this end, a renewed attention to the development of the regional initiatives is important. So far, the provision of different pathways into higher education and between HEIs has been identified as the most important objective. Collaborative research and innovation, which also have a space at the regional level, are underdeveloped. Progress in this direction requires a dialogue which includes research organisations other than HEIs. Their "voice" is needed in order to fully explore and exploit the opportunities related to regional initiatives, whose overall aim is to create dynamic and viable knowledge regions.

The commitment of the HEIs visited to the Regional Clusters and other regional initiatives was evident in many ways. On top of the strategic decisions which need to be appropriately informed, there is a need to set up teams to work on the development of possible ways of implementing decisions in a range of areas, including skills, research and local development. The organisational capacity of the institutions is crucial for achieving these common objectives as is the strengthening of the communication of strategic objectives and decisions across the HEIs and their regional partners.

At this point, it is worth taking a closer look into the governance requirements for these regional initiatives. The complexity and diversity of stakeholders makes knowledge management within them much more complex than within the closed system of HEIs. Hence, careful consideration needs to be given to management and governance systems. An example of an effective governance structure is the Shannon Consortium, which brings together the University of Limerick, the Limerick Institute of Technology, the Mary Immaculate College, local community and businesses, city and county councils (Box 3.1).

Box 3.1. Shannon Consortium

The Shannon Consortium was created in 2007 bringing together the University of Limerick (UL) and the Limerick Institute of Technology (LIT), the two key drivers of the consortium, which has developed into a vibrant HEI partnership, also involving Mary Immaculate College, local community and businesses, city and county councils.

The leadership in both the Limerick Institute of Technology and the University of Limerick has given substance, at a strategic level, to their joint attempts to help address regional development issues and shared services opportunities. Their actions manifest themselves as jointly grasped opportunities, strategic plan statements and public commitment to their region. The joint bid (together with other regional partners) to the Strategic Innovation Fund, an Irish government initiative, in 2006 to establish a Shannon Consortium, arose directly as a result of the close personal working relationship between the presidents of the two HEIs. The Chairperson of the Shannon Consortium is a retired senior civil servant and former diplomat from Limerick City.

The excellent collaboration between the HEIs has led to a growing number of innovative joint activities in education and research. Examples are a combined graduate school and PhD accreditation (which commenced in 2015), collaborative springboard courses as well as applied research activities and new, effective ways to enhance enterprise engagement (e.g. Limerick for IT). Sharing of rewards for joint supervision of theses is under discussion and there is a clear policy in place for students who wish to transfer from LIT to UL and vice versa after successfully completing the required number of programme modules. "Limerick for IT" is an IT skills partnership which commenced in 2014 and combines the strengths of the two HEIs in partnership with key industry partners, such as General Motors, Johnson & Johnson, Kerry Group, Limerick City and County Council and IDA Ireland. The initiative has facilitated

> Box 3.1. **Shannon Consortium** (cont.)
>
> attracting foreign direct investment and job creation which has also led to new forms of collaboration between higher education and industry (e.g. Johnson and Johnson Development Centre).
>
> The impact of the Shannon Consortium is significant. For example, the multinational company Northern Trust would not have chosen to locate in Limerick without the consortium being in place, which enabled fast response times to the development of staff training programmes, the provision of office space etc. This has led to 400 new jobs being located in Limerick.
>
> *Source:* HEInnovate (2015).

Evaluating the performance of the research system

Understanding and addressing the societal challenges of today's world requires contributions from all areas of knowledge. Innovation 2020, Ireland's strategy for research and development, science and technology, recognises the importance of continuing to support excellent research across all disciplines. Ireland needs to continue its commitment to investment in research taking into account the need for prioritisation and at the same time guaranteeing that all disciplines receive adequate funding and perform at the highest level. In 2015, an independent expert panel reviewed progress under the national research prioritisation exercise. Its recommendations include "research prioritisation should be positioned in a broader, strategic research framework which recognises the need to fund excellent research in other areas, in order to underpin the wider skills agenda, to meet broader societal goals and to further enhance Ireland's reputation for outstanding science" (DJEI, 2015).

Because there is no common research classification system funding agencies find it hard to share data on HEIs and researchers. If there was a common classification system and in as far as possible an agreed dataset to be collected (with additional indicators where required for particular agencies), then it would be much easier to build a common interface and share data.

There is a need to value the role and societal contributions of higher education. Irish HEIs need to be recognised for their important role, contributing not only to the qualifications of the work force at the highest level but also to social cohesion, economic development and growth. In other countries regular performance evaluations are conducted to allow for the provision of essential investment by the state in the maintenance and upgrading of the physical infrastructure, equipment and human capital to ensure continued performance of the research system.

Evaluating the performance of a research system is essential to its credibility but also in determining its impact and ability to attract continued investment. In Ireland there is no periodic and systematic evaluation of the performance of the research system. In the absence of a national assessment regime, some universities have undertaken internal reviews. Also, national funding agencies request information from HEIs and funded researchers periodically. For example, all SFI programmes have been reviewed by independent consultants and deemed fit for purpose. All SFI industry facing programmes have a core focus on commercialisation and innovation leading to economic impacts. Moreover, industry partnerships ensure the relevance of the research. However, all this does not replace a national evaluation exercise, which applies a common approach to all funders and evaluates research groups and not individual researchers according to performance and agreed contracts using international criteria and experts in order to ensure its continued performance, and the provision of essential investment by the state in human capital and in the maintenance of the physical infrastructure. Initiating such an approach should be considered.

A national evaluation exercise is a powerful instrument for improving the research system and for increasing its capacity to attract investment. Aside from determining performance it is also important for Ireland to determine a research unit's capability to continue as a high performer in terms of its human resources, capital infrastructure and any future investment. The aim is to support a research system, constituted by units that guarantee a good and growing level of critical mass and quality, involving professors, associated researchers, PhDs and post docs. These units should have a programme and plan of activities for a certain period of time (e.g. 5-6 years). Capital infrastructure and any future investment (floor funding) would be provided by the state. Core funding is addressed at maintaining the operational capacity of the research unit. At the same time, the steering of the system and the national priorities can be addressed with competitive calls.

An example of such a national evaluation exercise is the *Fundação para a Ciência e Tecnologia*, the Foundation for Science and Technology (FCT) in Portugal, which leads periodic external evaluation of the R&D units carried out by international experts (Box 3.2). In small countries, such as Ireland and Portugal, these assessments need to be carried out by international experts in order to avoid conflicts of interest.

Box 3.2. The periodic external evaluation of the R&D units in Portugal

In Portugal, every six years an external evaluation exercise is performed on the scientific and technological activities undertaken so far and planned for the next six years. The evaluation is organised by the *Fundação para a Ciência e Tecnologia* (FCT) and includes site visits by international teams, nominated by the FCT Board, applying a set of transparent evaluation criteria. Evaluation criteria are established to assess the scientific productivity and respective impact, contributions to the national scientific and technological system, merits of the research team and the quality and feasibility of the strategic plan. The impact of the scientific, technological and cultural output is also taken into consideration. Special attention is given to fields of study for which bibliometric data is not readily available, like the Arts, Humanities and Social Sciences.

The results are graded from "exceptional" to "excellent", "very good", "good" and "fair". Only research units that have passed the evaluation will receive state funding, which consists of two components: core funding and strategic funding. Core funding is allocated to units rated equal to or higher than "good", the amount provided reflects the size of the unit and its laboratory intensity. Additional strategic funding is allocated to units graded "excellent" or "exceptional". Funding is stopped for those units which do not achieve a certain standard.

The result of this exercise is also used by the HEIs' leadership to further enhance areas of strength and alternatively to close under-performing areas. Interdisciplinary units of considerable dimension were also created. These units address larger themes such as ageing, communication, etc. They compete for basic funding but also have funding from industry. An independent funding agency provides a programme for scholarships on a multi-annual basis with additional funding for temporary staff. The independent funding agency is also regularly evaluated.

> Box 3.2. **The periodic external evaluation of the R&D units in Portugal** *(cont.)*
>
> When the FCT was introduced, criticisms were raised about, amongst other things, the high costs and the fact that only high performing research units received funding and the resources to compete internationally, which simply resulted in the good ones becoming better. A further point of critique was also the undeniable fact that research competition has displaced the collegiate, collaborative values that the academic world once held. However, even if this is partially true, the level of competition generated from such an exercise is nothing compared to the competition generated by the worldwide rankings, which greatly influence the institutional capacity to attract talent.
>
> *Source:* Author's own work.

Organisational capacity from an institutional perspective

Government can enhance (or force) through competitive funding programmes the achievement of critical mass, interdisciplinarity and societal and economic relevance of education and research. At the same time, HEIs themselves can introduce measures which have these effects through allocation of funding, awards and other forms of individual or departmental incentives and rewards. All HEIs visited have excellent examples of these. They offer valuable learnings for other HEIs in Ireland and abroad and are presented in the following.

Dealing with decreasing funding for research and the search for new funding sources

The need to attain financial sustainability has led HEIs across Europe to become much more proactive in the search for new income streams. The net result is positive and Ireland is no exception, with HEIs increasing the number of funding sources. Some HEIs count more than 100 different sources of income (EUA, 2013). However, there are negative consequences of success in diversifying income. First is the need to meet the cost of compliance arising from different (and complex) accountability regimes and second is the need to be permanently on the lookout for new opportunities.

Several universities have set up offices to support researchers in making applications for funding and fulfilling reporting requirements. The HEIs visited have responded positively in terms of securing additional sources of funding and in linking external and internal sources of funding. Often this is easier for the universities than for the IOTs and smaller colleges that have more limited capacity.

Collaboration between HEIs also helps to secure greater funding. An example is the Irish Centre for Cloud Computing and Commerce (IC4). It was established in 2012 at Dublin City University (DCU) in collaboration with University College of Cork (UCC) and Athlone Institute of Technology. IC4 is also the largest contributor to innovation partnerships in the country. IC4 operates like a club; the current 45 members pay a small fee to participate in research projects and co-steer IC4's research agenda. To start a new project, at least two members need to state their intention to buy a non-exclusive license. Every four weeks formal all-member meetings are organised, with various informal and bilateral meetings in between. IC4 has targeted capacity building for SMEs. Support is provided for funding applications and in small applied research projects with SMEs up to 80% of the funding can be provided from IC4. In Innovation Voucher projects, the intellectual property is left with the company, which is apparently an exception in computing where the common approach is licensing.

According to its management, it is on track towards acquiring one-third of its budget from competitive funding; a milestone for its fifth year of existence.

A successful example of reorganising existing resources while demonstrating self-confidence and key strengths in focusing teaching, research and entrepreneurship on citizens, society and grand challenges is also provided by DCU. Four strategic research areas have been defined and mapped onto the national research priority areas. In the initial consultation process, a small number of staff from each department were released on a half-time basis to perform the analysis. The first goal of DCU's integrated strategy was to identify how to achieve an internal integration of staff focused on the creation of various interfaces between DCU and its stakeholder environment. The different skill sets required – e.g. technology knowledge, business development, commercialisation, marketing, and fundraising – were drawn from different parts of DCU (e.g. Invent, the Innovation and Enterprise Centre) and from newly hired staff.

A key initial challenge was to quickly build acceptance of a new type of structure. The Vice-President for Research steered the process and initiated a large-scale communication process to create commitment for the reallocation of resources within a new and broader framework (e.g. The Science and Technology Engagement Platform). The research office provides resources from an HEI-wide pool for each of the four strategic research themes and works closely with the implementing research teams. The research office supports principal investigators for a period of 12 to 18 months with guidance and mentoring, the development of impact case studies, and the handling of third-party funding. This has successfully raised the level of interaction and introduced a more interdisciplinary framework. The aim in the near future is to enhance the internal capacities through the development of an overarching support team which will cover various common areas, and use more efficiently specific expertise, such as dealing with the administration of EU funding, providing training sessions for staff, and ensuring a interdisciplinary approach is taken to research proposals and activities. Plans exist to deploy a DCU staff member to Brussels to liaise closely with research officers in the European Commission.

Incentivising innovation and knowledge exchange

Current pay structures and employment conditions within the Irish higher education system do not allow for bonus payments or other financial rewards for those who actively support the HEI's entrepreneurial agenda other than where a share of the sale of intellectual property has been agreed. Individual HEIs, however, do provide other incentives including reduction in teaching loads (not possible in IOTs), in support of, for example, R&D activities. For example, in the University of Limerick (UL), third mission activities are considered part of the workload allocation model and are taken into account when promotional opportunities arise.

Irish HEIs stimulate staff and students to demonstrate excellence in education, research and societal engagement. All of the HEIs visited have President's awards for this. At DCU achievements in industry engagement and dialogue with society are also recognised for promotional purposes, and four annual President's awards recognise outstanding achievements in teaching and learning, research, engagement, and innovation. In particular, the latter has seen high numbers of applications from administrative and support staff. At UCC, significant efforts are underway to encourage and recognise staff and students who make an impact at institutional, local and national levels. The Staff Development Committee has introduced a range of programmes focused on staff motivation and staff recognition, which have proven to be important in attracting and retaining staff. One of these, the Staff Recognition Awards Programme, is now in its sixth year. In 2015, fourteen awards were available in five categories including: The Frank McGrath Perpetual Award for Equality and Welfare, the Impact Award, the Leadership Award, Exceptional Citizen Award, Enhancing the Student Experience Award, and Outstanding Colleague. Two impact awards were also developed to recognise achievements in the Arts, Humanities and Social Sciences (AHSS), and in Science, Technology, Engineering and Mathematics (STEM) fields. So far, no specific award has been considered which would recognise interdisciplinary achievements.

The collaboration between HEIs in Limerick through the Shannon Consortium (Box 3.2, above) has led to a growing number of innovative joint activities in education and research. The recent mapping of academic programmes identified several common areas. Different ways of organising joint delivery evenly and equitably across the binary system are currently being reviewed by the faculty heads in order to find solutions to overcome logistical challenges including the movement of students across the city for tuition at different campuses, the establishing of new classroom technologies to enable distance and online education and dealing with barriers in the recurrent grant allocation model (RGAM). This was deliberately organised at departmental level and not at senior management level in order to reach out to as many staff as possible. Regular two-hour workshops are organised for staff to exchange experience and to build awareness and skills around key issues, such as facilitating group work, assessment in experiential learning and others.

There are also examples of cases where delays and bottlenecks in capital development have led to office sharing arrangements across faculties and the mixing of staff from different disciplines within shared office space, which, in turn, have spurred organisational innovation. For example, this was the case at the Galway Mayo Institute of Technology. While not deliberately planned or intended this interdisciplinary mixing has resulted in more informal interaction amongst staff from different faculties, and subsequently more interdisciplinary collaboration including new interdisciplinary initiatives in teaching and research. Efforts are underway to further spread this as a practice to enhance structures and mechanisms for cross-department communication.

Conclusions

Ireland's social and economic fabric needs a robust system for transforming knowledge into action. Many elements are already in place and well developed. Education, research, and innovation all combine together to create growth and social cohesion if promoted by talented people and supported by adequate policy. Investment is needed in all three components. Funding just one area will not be enough, like the pistons of an engine, all need to be properly maintained. Vital will be a quadruple helix bringing together HEIs, business, government and civil society.

Regional collaborative initiatives involving HEIs, such as the Regional Clusters and the Regional Skills Fora, are not only the building blocks of the 21st century Higher Education System in Ireland but the initial stage for the development of knowledge and innovation regions in Ireland and as such it is timely to devote renewed attention to the initiatives. To achieve the overall aim of these initiatives requires strengthening research capacity and capability, promoting enterprise and innovation, and attracting and retaining talent from home and abroad. A future phase in regional initiatives needs to focus on knowledge producers, users and transformers from businesses, industry and civil society. The buy-in from all HEIs involved in regional initiatives will be of utmost importance for their success. Strong, clear and non-excessive governance arrangements are essential.

The research prioritisation exercise saw a greater emphasis on the impact of research and its relevance to the enterprise base. Addressing societal challenges increasingly requires interisciplinary collaboration between medical, technological and scientific research interwoven with research questions and practices from all fields. This could be strengthened, for example, in the form of special calls developed for research programmes and projects that promote inter- and transdisciplinary collaborations. Innovation 2020, Ireland's strategy for research and development, science and technology, is a good platform which recognises the importance of continuing to support excellent research across all disciplines.

The introduction of a national evaluation exercise, which applies a common approach to all funders and evaluates research groups and not individual researchers according to performance and agreed contracts using international criteria and experts would be a way to ensure the provision of essential state investment in human capital and physical infrastructure, and, in turn, a continued performance of the research system in Irish higher education.

Finally, mobility opportunities for research staff, including academics, into industry and vice versa with a view to enhancing in-firm capabilities and university business knowledge links are important to strengthen entrepreneurship and innovation in Irish higher education. A framework for bi-directional movement of personnel from industry/academia may warrant consideration.

Notes

1. In Irish higher education mature learners are students that are at least 23 years of age at the time they enter the study programme.
2. See EUA (2013) for an overview and details of strategies used for funding European universities.
3. OECD, 2015 Based on OECD, *National Accounts Database*, ISIC Rev.4; Eurostat, National Accounts Statistics and national sources, April 2015. http://dx.doi.org/10.1787/888933224376.

References

EUA (2013), *Designing Strategies for Efficient Funding of Higher Education in Europe*, European University Association, Brussels.

EUA (2015), DEFINE *Thematic Report: University Mergers in Europe*, published online, www.eua.be/Libraries/publications-homepage-list/DEFINE_Thematic_Report_2_University_Mergers_in_Europe_final (accessed 11 February 2017).

European Commission (2015), *The Knowledge Future: Intelligent Policy Choices for Europe 2050*, Brussels, published online, www.ec.europa.eu/research/foresight/pdf/knowledge_future_2050.pdf (accessed 11 February 2017).

Department of Enterprise, Jobs and Innovation (2015), *Review of Progress in Implementing Research Prioritisation. Report of the Independent Panel*, published online, https://www.djei.ie/en/Publications/Publication-files/Review-of-Progress-Research-Prioritisation.pdf (accessed 11 February 2017).

HEInnovate (2017), "Shared governance, leadership and regional development: A case study", www.heinnovate.eu/sites/default/files/shared_governance_leadership_and_regional_development_-_a_case_study.pdf (accessed 11 February 2017).

OECD (2015), *OECD Digital Economy Outlook*, OECD Publishing, Paris, www.dx.doi.org/10.1787/888933224376 (accessed 11 February 2017).

Chapter 4

Building entrepreneurial capacity through teaching and learning

This chapter expands on the findings presented in Chapter 2 with a focus on teaching and learning. It gives an overview of the national level approaches and initiatives in this regard, namely the teaching and learning recommendations in the National Strategy for Higher Education to 2030 and the establishment of the National Forum for the Enhancement of Teaching & Learning in Higher Education. The chapter analyses various approaches to enhance the capacity of students for entrepreneurship and reviews the role of higher education institutions in lifelong learning. The chapter also discusses the role of education in translating scientific research into societal relevance and presents good practice examples of how to incentivise student participation in knowledge exchange activities.

Introduction

Teaching and learning are central activities of higher education institutions (HEIs). Former boundaries to researchers and societal engagement are starting to blur and new synergies are emerging. Quickly emerging new modes of learning are putting traditional approaches in education to the test. The "flipped" classroom, in which teachers and students occupy changing roles in teaching and learning, is an umbrella concept for the emerging practical applications of the need to rethink the education mode (OECD, 2006). At the same time, there is a growing societal demand for HEIs to translate research results for and communicate them with the wider public. No single HEI, and indeed the higher education sector as a whole, can any longer claim the paramount discovery and repository of knowledge. HEIs in their responses to this shift seek to expand their organisational capacity around useful and problem-centred sources of knowledge, making space for transdisciplinary research to discover, explore, co-create and disseminate knowledge in novel ways (Armbruster, 2008).

Across the globe, acceptance for the shared responsibility in ensuring graduate employability is growing and the expected role for HEIs in this is to provide a balanced combination of knowledge and practical skills. Government funding for higher education is getting increasingly tied to demonstrated impact of education on the transformation of learners into, what in public discourse is called "T-shaped professionals", with cutting-edge and deep discipline-specific knowledge as well as a broad set of cognitive, non-cognitive and metacognitive skills. This combination of knowledge and skills is what helps individuals to demonstrate initiative, rely on judgement, while showing empathy and taking into account possible consequences, learning via trial and error processes, and creating own job environments. Often, these attributes are used to describe an entrepreneur (Frese, 2009). Building on this broader understanding of an entrepreneur, in 2008, the European Commission launched a large-scale initiative to promote the sense of initiative and entrepreneurship as one of eight transversal competencies, which can and should be developed through formal education and lifelong learning activities. In response, many governments have given HEIs a (funded) mandate for this.

Analysis and findings

Ireland's systemic approach to enhance excellence in teaching and learning

With 60% tertiary attainment amongst the age group 30-34 years by 2020, Ireland has set itself the second highest EU2020 goal within the European Union.[1] Since 2003, the country has been moving steadily towards this target from an initial 35.1% to 52.3% in 2015. Ireland has very favourable demographics with the highest proportion of the population under the age of 15 in the European Union. Students participating in higher education are expected to grow by nearly 30% over the next 15 years, from a current base of 215 000 (DES, 2015).

To facilitate the growth of Irish higher education, the National Strategy for Higher Education to 2030 provides a set of recommendations. The aim is to create the framework conditions, which allow HEIs to respond effectively to the increasing industry demand for high-order knowledge-based skills, the changing profile of students, and the need to render research more relevant for development and growth. With regard to teaching and learning, eight recommendations were put forward; several of which have been widely or fully achieved to date (Figure 4.1).

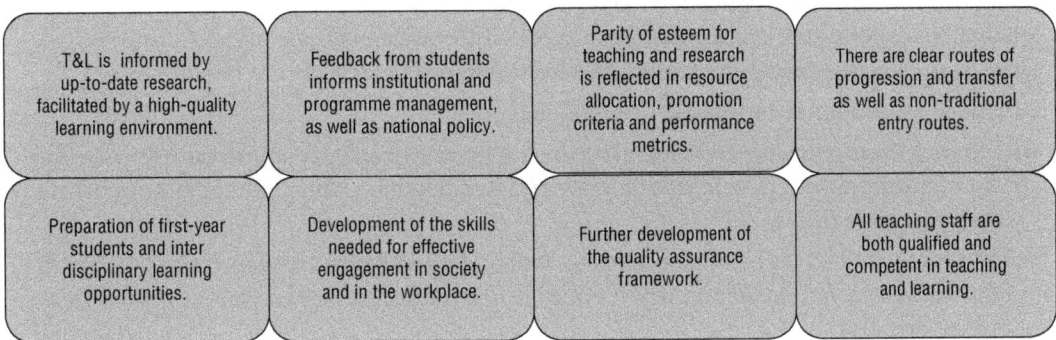

Figure 4.1. **Teaching and learning recommendations in the Irish Higher Education Strategy**

Source: DES (2011).

Significant efforts are underway to allocate resources and develop performance metrics which reflect the parity of esteem between teaching and research. A new annual survey of student engagement provides feedback to institutions and is reported on at national level.

The expansion of places in higher education has also provided more opportunities for young people from disadvantaged backgrounds. Aside from standard entry routes, there has been an increased focus in recent years on lifelong learners through initiatives such as the ICT Conversion Courses and the Springboard Programme (see Chapter 1). The provision of academic, social supports and guidance that enhance the motivation, engagement and performance of students, as well as collaboration between the HEIs and further education providers has helped create new pathways.

The National Framework of Qualifications provides with the multi-ladder system several routes of access, progression and transfer with credited exit routes and re-entry options (see Chapter 1). This is particularly well received, by mature students who have a greater need to achieve a balance between their work, family and educational lives, as well as by employers who want to offer their staff flexible educational opportunities. Increased focus on recognition of prior learning also benefits these students.

Various initiatives are underway to better prepare first-year students for their academic learning experience and enhanced emphasis is given to the development of skills required for effective engagement in society and in the workplace. The quality assurance framework has been reviewed and further developed, involving subject experts from the academic community under the co-ordination of Quality and Qualifications Ireland (QQI). As part of this, all HEIs are expected to offer development support and training opportunities for their teaching staff.

To support HEIs in ensuring that every teacher has an opportunity to contribute to the change processes in education, in 2012 the Irish government introduced the National Forum for the Enhancement of Teaching & Learning in Higher Education (Box 4.1). The National

> **Box 4.1. Ireland's National Forum for the Enhancement of Teaching & Learning in Higher Education**
>
> The National Forum for the Enhancement of Teaching & Learning in Higher Education was established in 2012 by the Minister for Education and Skills to enhance the quality of the learning experience for all students in higher education, be they full-time, part-time or flexible learners. The National Forum maintains a continuous dialogue with students, teachers and managers in all higher education institutions in order to shape the future directions of the higher education sector in Ireland (e.g. "Teaching for Transitions"). HEI leaders, managers, staff and students are involved through positions in the Forum's board, awards, such as the teaching heroes (see below) and act as local Forum contact points.
>
> To date, the National Forum has undertaken:
>
> - A comprehensive review of digital platforms, e-learning capacity across the entire sector and of professional development activities for teachers and managers supporting teaching and learning;
> - A student-led teaching award programme, which is an evidence-based professional award fellowship system subsequently feeding into a national professional development framework; and
> - A series of research and dissemination activities in the form of reports, insights, talks, jointly organised seminars and other events and scholarships.
>
> *Source:* Interviews with representatives of the National Forum for the Enhancement of Teaching & Learning in Higher Education in Ireland during the study visit in October 2015.

Forum is a sectoral network which pools resources and efforts directed at advocacy, connecting excellent practice, collaboration, and the mobilisation of expertise. It is an important stepping stone in connecting, developing and mainstreaming already existing and new initiatives.

The National Forum collaborates regularly with one or more HEIs for the organisation of research and dissemination seminars. These events focus on student engagement and learning techniques to promote more effective teaching. Typically, these events are a combination of lectures, demonstrations and workshops. A recurring focus has been on innovation in assessment approaches, for example, the exploration and articulation of mental models, which steer the teacher's understanding of assessment and its impacts on the students' learning.

Students and staff from all HEIs are involved in a new award which identifies and celebrates student-nominated teaching excellences. The Teaching Hero Award, started in 2014, is the only student-led national teaching award in Ireland. The awards are a collaborative effort of the National Forum and the Union of Students in Ireland. The 2016 theme of "Inspiring and Innovating" asked students to identify teachers who have engaged with new ideas and practices to enhance their learning experience resulting in 800 nominations and 37 award winners.

Engagement and knowledge exchange activities in higher education

Engagement can be an important catalyst for organisational innovation, the advancement of education and research, and local development. HEIs play several roles in their communities and one of their key functions is to support and drive regional, social and community development; they are a force for social transformation. HEIs are often one of the major employers in a locality and by their existence will impact on the local economy and social wellbeing. Their impact is universally recognised in this context (see Chapter 5).

As societal, economic and cultural themes change over time, the research system has a key role to play in the process of reflection, analysis and charting future paths. Not only the content of research, but the manner in which the research is conducted is arguably equally important to ensure good outcomes. The Irish University Association and the Irish Research Council have documented a wide range of research initiatives in Irish universities that fulfil these central premises (IUA and IRC, 2016).

An entrepreneurial HEI is a highly active player with a strong presence in the community. The HEIs visited and reviewed as part of this report all demonstrate excellent and promising practices across these aspects. An example is the Galway Mayo Institute of Technology (GMIT). Since its establishment in the early 1970s GMIT has been one of the principal providers of higher education in Galway city and the western region. It has a strong, well-established and widely recognised tradition in innovative academic programmes, applied research and development activities and engagement initiatives which have contributed greatly to the economic, social and cultural development of the region. With its regional distribution there are many parts of a large rural area that GMIT has reached out to using community based outreach approaches. As part of an inclusive education strategy, GMIT is working with further education providers in the region on course development, as well as on student transfer and progression arrangements.

Some of the current local and community initiatives include GMIT's voluntary student teaching programme, which commenced in 2003 and was designed to get students involved in teaching in local primary schools. Junior Achievement Ireland provided the training for this. GMIT has already begun enrolling some students who experienced this programme during their primary education and who were taught by the approximately 500 GMIT alumni involved in the initiative (Box 4.2). From this initiative, a wide range of social enterprise activities were also spun out. GMIT has developed a social enterprise module whose use across the HEI is growing. Also worth mentioning is the CANSAS project in mechanical engineering, which allows students to interact with secondary school pupils with a view to raising interest in science and technology through a project focused on designing and developing a mini-satellite.

Box 4.2. Junior Teaching Ireland at the Galway Mayo Institute of Technology

In 1995, Ireland joined Junior Achievement, a global initiative for the development of entrepreneurial skills amongst students in primary and secondary education. The Galway Mayo Institute of Technology (GMIT) has become Ireland's Midwest crucible of the Junior Achievement global initiative.

Junior Teaching Ireland is a voluntary teaching initiative which started at GMIT in 2003. Students in their fourth year, who are enrolled in an entrepreneurship course, go out to primary and second-level schools and teach younger kids. Over 12 000 primary school children took part. This year GMIT welcomed first year students who first heard about GMIT when they were themselves in secondary education and experienced as pupils the Junior Teaching initiative.

Source: Interviews at Galway Mayo Institute of Technology during the study visit in October 2015.

In Limerick, the excellent collaboration between the University of Limerick (UL) and the Limerick Institute of Technology (LIT) has led to a growing number of innovative joint activities in education and research (see also Chapter 3). Key to the success of this partnership is the joint commitment of the two HEIs to regional development, complementarity and trust. Educational outreach initiatives of note include Limerick for IT (Box 4.4), and Limerick for Engineering which target second-level school pupils and their parents with activities such as "Engineering weeks", "Engineer for a day", and the "Open days for parents". These are particularly promising initiatives to promote Science, Technology, Engineering and Mathematics (STEM) subjects amongst female pupils. Also, several activities are underway to promote interest in information and communications technology (ICT) programmes and awareness of the industry and related career opportunities. Since 2012, LIT senior management has promoted the national Coder Dojo initiative, with workshops organised on campus at weekends for children from primary and second-level schools. The programme is delivered by volunteers from industry as well as LIT students.

LIT wants to become Ireland's most accessible HEI. Currently 30% of newly enrolled students are mature learners and the percentage of students that receive a state grant is above the national average (65% versus 45% nationally). LIT has also enrolled double the national average of students with a disability (9%). Existing pathways from further education providers, via the various agreements signed with its surrounding education and training boards, are noteworthy. For example, in art and design programmes the transition from further to higher education is facilitated by providing students with a common first year as a kind of "diagnostic phase" where students can work out where their specific interests lie. In particular, the community activities under development by LIT in Moyross are a promising avenue to increase participation in higher education in a community where it was almost non-existent (see below).

The role of education in translating scientific research into societal relevance

A common demand of research is that it is of high scientific quality and that it is relevant to society. Whereas the first part of the demand is incontrovertible and central to the assessment of research proposals as well as the evaluation of academic research, the second part concerning the societal relevance of research, however, is not self-evident. To follow the argumentation it is useful to differentiate between the process of research and its outcomes. The latter are subject to circumstances that go beyond the control of the researcher, unlike the research process, in which the researcher formulates the research questions. This process should, as Bouter (2008) reminds us, "always be accompanied by a reflection on the expectations in terms of relevance to society".

A notable initiative in this regard is CARL, the Community-Academic Research Links initiative at UCC. Since 2010, important pieces of research have been produced and implemented, some of which have impacted also on national policy. CARL researchers work with not-for-profit voluntary and community organisations on a range of research topics. Selected research projects are intended to result in practical applications. One example of this is a checklist for Munchausen Syndrome patients, which can be used by family members and care personnel as a first diagnosis tool. As part of the research agreement, students, community partners and UCC academics agree that completed research reports are posted online. CARL is now extending its activities within all four colleges of UCC.

The University of Limerick (UL) has commenced with the development of case studies on research impact. To this end, the Vice-President for Research has brought together groups of researchers from different faculties and worked with them in order to develop an understanding of "what" impact is and "how" it can be measured. This is an excellent example of emerging good practice which could be mainstreamed across the Irish higher education system and abroad. It includes the preparation of case studies and stories about the impact of some of the research and, how and where this can be demonstrated, for example by translating research findings into practical guidelines and tracking the practical implications of using those guidelines on developments in policy design and implementation. Training is offered and templates are available to raise impact awareness and thinking when formulating research activities. UL is actively working on its impact agenda in anticipation of a greater focus in this area. This comes in response to and in anticipation of the wider trends of the impact agenda (in Europe through the Horizon 2020 funding, and in the United Kingdom with the Research Excellence Framework), rather than being reactive to any future developments in Ireland in terms of a possible impact "policy".

Enhancing student participation in knowledge exchange activities

In general, providing incentives and removing administrative barriers are fundamental for raising the interest of students to participate in knowledge exchange activities. There are several obvious reasons to engage in these activities, for example, gaining experience and contacts, European Credit Transfer and Accumulation System (ECTS), etc. Depending on the intensity and duration of these activities, students may, however, also encounter administrative barriers. For example, additional work placements or starting up a business might require a suspension of studies or an extension of the enrolment period, which might not be compliant with existing study regulations. There are various learning points from the HEIs visited.

Many staff members of the Limerick Institute of Technology (LIT) sit on community partnership boards and students are encouraged to get involved in volunteer work, for example through GIVE, an all-campus initiative, in which students commit hours to voluntary work (e.g. 6 000 hours in the last academic year). An HEI-wide database exists which records which external boards and community groups staff are members of. A President's award recognises staff and students for their community outreach and engagement activities. In particular, the community activities under development by LIT in Moyross are a promising opportunity to increase participation in higher education in a community where it was almost non-existent. At present, on the northern part of the LIT campus a wall of about three meters height separates student housing from the Moyross neighbourhood. This has created a physical distance, which – paired with social distance (Boudon, 1974) – negatively affects perceptions of the feasibility and desirability of (higher) educational options. Children living in Moyross are aware of the distance between the academic world and their own. LIT has recognised the wall's symbolic dimension (it reaches a height of four metres in places) and is working with Limerick City Council administration towards its removal. In the meantime, the wall could be used for artistic expressions, giving LIT students and youngsters from Moyross an opportunity to engage in community work and to transform the wall into a symbol of collaboration and pathways into higher education.

A notable initiative, which provides students with recognition for achievements during work placements, is the UCC Works Award. Introduced in 2012, it offers a diploma supplement and an award for outstanding achievements for students who undertake either a campus student/work placement, volunteer with a not-for-profit organisation or become an active member of a student society at UCC for a minimum of 40 hours. UCC

Works providers can sign up online by providing a letter of interest. They are expected to allocate a supervisor/mentor to support and mentor students, ensure that students have a sufficient level of responsibility to learn the required employability skills from the experience, and provide students with clear written documentation outlining their duties, goals, learning objectives, supervision arrangements and work schedule. The career service supports UCC Works providers in this process.

A similar initiative is underway at Dublin City University (DCU). The Uaneen Module formally recognises and rewards students for their "external" achievements and meaningful contributions to campus life. It is managed and administered by DCU's Student Life Office. It dates back to 2000 and since 2004 up to five ECTS credits can be awarded to students on Diploma Supplements in recognition of 125 hours participation in relevant external or campus life activities. Assessment is based on a learning diary submitted by the student. Students who achieve a First Class honour in the Uaneen Module and who, additionally, achieve a First Class honours result in their degree, are considered for nomination for the Chancellor's Medal.

Work placements

Multinational corporations often have structured programmes for the early identification of future employees and, to this end, make use of work placements and co-operative education arrangements. In contrast, small and medium-sized enterprises (SMEs) often lack a good understanding of the (contractual) opportunities and their implications. This is backed up by the results from the 2015 National Employer Survey, which covered employer organisations of various sizes and sectors and accounting for an estimated 12% of the total graduate recruitment. Large and/or foreign owned companies were found to be more likely to establish a relationship with an education provider to source graduates than small organisations (71% versus 42%). The primary reasons for establishing a relationship with an HEI as a source of future graduates were: near proximity, existing relationships with previous graduates who are now employees, and specific offerings such as internships, placements and work experience programmes (HEA et al., 2015). The National Skills Strategy includes actions and targets for increasing work placements (DES, 2016).

Promoting the opportunities around work placements and co-operative education and building a good understanding of the implications and benefits are central tasks for the career services in HEIs. In particular SMEs will welcome such support as it reduces the firm's costs and resource allocation. An effective organisation of work placements requires the HEI's support, centrally and at department level, in terms of i) sharing information internally because host organisations prefer to have single interlocutors, ii) facilitating the supervision of students, especially related to academic requirements and co-tutorship arrangements, iii) providing assistance to the intern during the work placement, iv) making sure that experience reports cover the twin objectives of supporting the student in reflecting on the learning experience, and informing other students and teachers about it.

All HEIs in Ireland recognise the enormous value of co-operative education for student learning, strategic research collaboration and professional education. Recent policy analysis and advice work carried out by the "Roadmap for Employment-Academic Partnership"[2] (REAP) project, funded through the Higher Education Authority (HEA), developed a model for co-operative learning arrangements. REAP helped to establish the following responsibilities and commitment in co-operative learning arrangements for HEIs, students and employers (Figure 4.2).

Figure 4.2. **Organisation of co-operative learning in Irish HEIs**

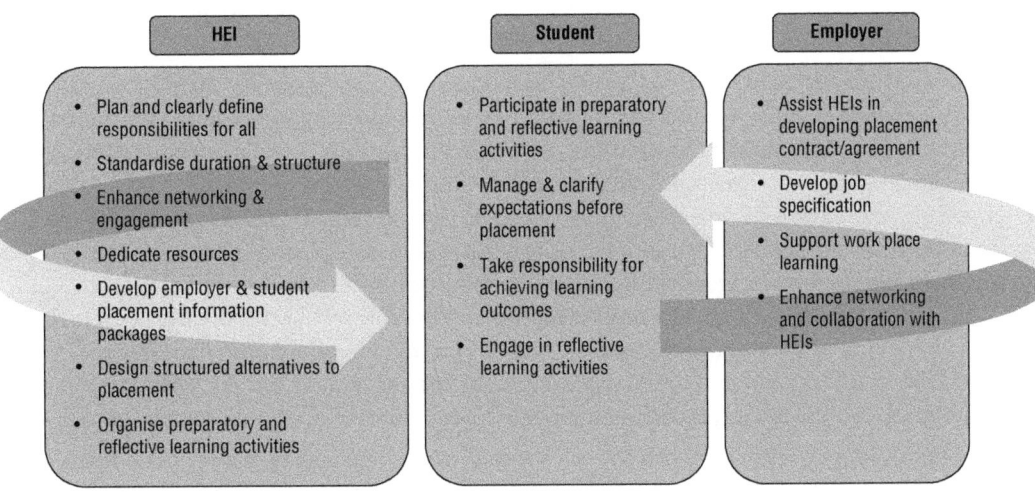

Source: Author's own work, adapted from Sheridan and Linehan (2011).

At the University of Limerick, co-operative education is considered crucial for creating dialogue and partnerships with employers and has led to a range of extensive forms of collaboration with industry. To this end, problem-based learning is an underpinning educational principle at UL. The aim is to offer students, from early on in their studies, multiple opportunities to experience problem-based learning, despite high student-staff ratios in some of the courses. Every student spends at least six months in a work placement environment. Work placement opportunities are also available in incubator firms. UL's incubation and business acceleration facility also supports new entrepreneurs in the organisation of work placements, so that these work placements are as fruitful as the learning experiences provided in established local firms or multinational corporations.

LIT is the only HEI in Ireland which offers a full year of work placement as part of its Level 8 (Honours degree programme) in construction. Of particular note is the work-based learning support provided for third-year students in the Built Environment department as part of their year-long placement in industry (Box 4.3). An electronic diary has been developed for students to record tasks and to monitor the development of their competencies while in the work environment. This allows supervisors to quickly analyse what tasks are undertaken by students and the progress they are making. The competencies that students should gain while on placement were defined by the department. The department also publishes regular reports on the needs of the construction industry in the region, gathering skills requirements data from alumni contacts who now hold key positions in the industry.

Workplace opportunities are also a central element of education at UCC and are provided in the majority of undergraduate programmes. Pre-placement preparation is available in the form of extra-curricular weekly placement classes, in which students are coached in preparing their curriculum vitae and reviewing those of their peers. Speed networking events are also organised to coach students for interviews. These activities have been appraised by both students and employers as very effective in lowering the number of unsuccessful interviews. Replication across all colleges, with smaller group sizes, could be considered, and a similar initiative to support reflection upon learning during work

> ### Box 4.3. **Electronic diaries for co-operative learning at Limerick Institute of Technology**
>
> The Limerick Institute of Technology (LIT) offers the largest specialised centre for property, quantity surveying, and construction, as well as civil engineering education and training, outside of Dublin. Students in the Honours degree programme on Built Environment, offered by the School of the Built Environment have a year-long placement in construction and civil engineering companies during their third year. For this period, the school seeks to find a balance between the needs of student and employer. While it is important for the employer to immerse the student in practical learning experiences on the job, it is also important for the School of the Built Environment to record competency-based learning which the academic mentor can supervise. A solution was found in using electronic diaries. Students are required to fill in an electronic diary throughout the placement period. With this diary, they can record online what they learn, in terms of competencies or other learning instances.
>
> Teachers have real-time access to the diaries and can continuously monitor the learning progress of their students, in addition to the on-the-spot monitoring as part of arranged visits. Furthermore, the online dairies are recorded and thus immediately and automatically saved which makes tracking of students' activities and learning easier and more accessible for the teachers. In the online diaries particular attention is given to the development of soft skills. This has had a positive impact on the employability of students. The diary method has contributed to this by making supervision of students easier and making it possible to track their development in real-time. Teachers are able to react to what they find worthy of reflective intervention with the student. Also, students train their reflection and writing skills.
>
> Enrolment numbers have remained steady throughout the years of the economic crisis despite the reduced level of activity in the construction industry. This is due, in part, to applicants from a trade background taking the opportunity to achieve a higher level qualification suited to managerial level positions.
>
> Source: Interviews at Limerick Institute of Technology during the study visit in October 2015.

placement could be introduced replacing the debriefing session in the fourth year, which is too short and often held with too large a group to allow for full reflection and peer learning.

At DCU, an interesting approach to enhance peer learning and reflection is the Structured Mentorship Programme, co-organised by DCU Alumni and the Career Service. The programme runs for six-months between October and March and pairs second-year students with alumni mentors for the purposes of career and personal development. Alumni and students are matched based on their areas of professional expertise, DCU course and areas of interest. Alumni mentors are asked, if possible, to provide their student mentee with a work-shadowing day as part of the programme. Structured Mentorship involves a number of events on campus for both mentors and mentees. Mentors apply through the Alumni Office, and the Careers Service puts out the call to the students. Employers value highly the experience which students gain from this initiative in view of their expected effectiveness of the learning experience when connecting the graduate to somebody in the company who would help him/her learn.

Meeting the needs of employers and students

According to the 2015 National Employer Survey, in terms of satisfaction, employers were very satisfied with graduate recruits across a range of workplace and personal attributes. These included ICT skills, teamwork, communication, adaptability and flexibility, positive attitude and energy. A lower level of satisfaction was noted for foreign language capability, entrepreneurial skills and business acumen/awareness.

Approximately 40% of employer organisations indicated that there were skills not currently available that are required now or in the next five years. The main skills cited were engineering, languages, ICT and specific quantitative skills.

All HEIs visited are involved in embedding enhanced employability skills across all programmes and many have identified distinctive graduate attributes related to the particular teaching and learning strategies and programmes of the institution. Several learnings emerge from the reviewed practices. The core mission of DCU is based on four pillars: Transformation, Enterprise, Translation and Engagement. This reflects clearly the commitment towards enhancing the transformation of individuals and organisational structures, understood as one of the largest impacts of higher education, which cannot be captured by simple metrics. DCU's senior management have started to look for options to document transformational processes. As a result, all undergraduate students have individual e-portfolios. DCU is a forerunner in this field. A number of institutions are developing an e-portfolio approach to allow students to have attestation of generic skills acquired throughout the full duration of their undergraduate and postgraduate programmes. The National Forum for the Enhancement of Teaching & Learning in Higher Education has recently started to promote the introduction of e-portfolios widely across the Irish higher education sector.

At DCU, students can use their e-portfolio to monitor personal development in the following six key attributes: i) Creative and Enterprising, i.e. being innovative and problem-solving as well as adaptable and willing to pursue new ideas; ii) Solution-Oriented; iii) Effective Communicators, that is, to negotiate effectively, to collaborate, and to influence others; iv) Globally Engaged, in terms of being locally and globally aware, to value tolerance and cultural diversity, and to be committed to civic engagement; v) Active Leaders; and, vi) Committed to Continuous Learning in the spirit of inquiry, reflection and evaluation. Support is offered in the form of workshops and online resources. DCU alumni can keep their e-portfolios to use in their on-going development.

Another example is BEST (Building Education Success Together), an intensive introductory course at DCU, organised for first year students one week prior to the start of lectures, in all Business School programmes and in some programmes of the School of Applied Language and Intercultural Studies. Students learn team-working skills, reflect upon their learning styles, familiarise themselves with the Campus and get to know their classmates in a relaxed environment. Part of the BEST programme is a computer-based business simulation game, in which students make decisions about running a virtual chocolate company. The team that wins is the one which has made a significant profit on their investment. A conceptual broadening of this exercise could be considered, for example, by looking into the socio-economic and environmental impacts of their decisions along the production chain. BEST is a notable initiative in terms of building awareness and commitment to DCU's four strategy pillars. An expansion across all faculties and bringing together students from different schools and departments could also be considered.

Dundalk Institute of Technology has also, for a long time, championed the development of entrepreneurial mindsets and behaviours amongst staff and students and this is manifested in a variety of innovative programmes and initiatives. These include paperclip challenges, smartphone app competitions, a peer to peer student entrepreneurship enterprise programme and the development of a BSc in Engineering Entrepreneurship.

Learning beyond traditional lecture hall settings

Learning goes beyond traditional lecture hall settings, and is moving into a more digital world within the classroom and beyond, on and off campus. All HEIs in Ireland support flexible and blended learning, corresponding with the national objective to enhance the flexibility and responsiveness of higher education through the provision of open and distance learning as significant elements of study programmes.

An example is the Open Education Unit programme at DCU championed by internationally recognised academics. It offers several blended learning programmes designed to suit mature and international students who already have the capability to learn online. These programmes provide a much deeper and wider focus than distance learning and enable students to feel as close and engaged as on-campus students do. Negotiations are underway with HEIs in China to develop a course that prepares students studying in China with a locally tailored curriculum to continue their education at DCU.

One way to expand the suite of digital courses and modules across a wide range of study programmes is to assist academic teams, through the deployment of specialist technological staff, to aid in the design and development of digital course elements. Also, the work of those, who have pioneered such technologies in their teaching, should be analysed in order to learn from what they have done, and to work out support mechanisms for others who would benefit from deploying such technologies. Similarly, the time involved in developing video lectures etc. must be realistically assessed, and staff allocated the appropriate period of time during their working week (i.e. to develop one hour of a video lecture takes considerably more time to develop than an hour of a lecture to be delivered in person).

Lifelong learning

The Irish higher education sector has great growth potential in lifelong learning and continuous professional development. In the last decade, HEIs have, with some exceptions, focused primarily on the traditional 18-24 year old student (due in no small part to demographics) and in providing upskilling and reskilling opportunities for the unemployed. There is a growing recognition that more opportunities need to be provided for those already in employment to upskill and reskill to stay in employment, change career or start their own business. The Limerick for IT initiative, implemented jointly by the University of Limerick and Limerick Institute of Technology is an example of the provision of lifelong learning opportunities (Box 4.4).

With national level initiatives, such as the Springboard Programme (see Chapter 1), efforts have been enhanced to create financial and policy incentives for HEIs to organise lifelong learning. Initially, the focus was on the unemployed. Eligibility for programmes is being widened given the fall in unemployment. The Centre for Adult Continuing Education (ACE) at UCC is an example of how Irish HEIs have engaged in lifelong learning activities. Having a dynamic and responsive unit currently with 20 full-time staff has proven to be crucial in allowing ACE to offer its all-round service from programme writing and academic approval processes, to staffing arrangements and the recruitment of participants. Initially an intensive consultation process was undertaken to gather information about local employer needs. Close collaboration with UCC senior management helped to streamline the programme approval process and to introduce cost sharing mechanisms. This helped to raise interest at departmental level and academic participation in teaching the programmes, particularly amongst early career staff.

> **Box 4.4. The Limerick for IT initiative**
>
> The strategic development plan for Limerick city and the wider region, Limerick 2030, identified the need for an information technology (IT) skills framework that will enable job creation and leverage the knowledge based economic potential of Limerick, given the dominance of the IT sector in the region. In January 2014 major industry in the Limerick region, including General Motors, Johnson & Johnson and Kerry Group, together with the University of Limerick, the Limerick Institute of Technology, Limerick City & County Council and IDA Ireland, formed a unique IT skills partnership "Limerick for IT".
>
> The primary focus was to lead an employer-led skills specific project that would assess future skills needs in order for multinationals to secure further operational mandates and activities, thereby creating a virtuous circle of emerging skills and jobs. Therefore, the key role of the partnership was to build a pipeline of job-ready IT graduates to meet global and national needs.
>
> The first task of the group was to identify critical skills that could expand operation mandates. As a result, tailored education and reskilling programmes were developed and delivered through the University of Limerick and the Limerick Institute of Technology. This has resulted in two major expansions in Limerick with the creation of over 200 jobs since January 2014 and with potential for a further 1 000 jobs over the next three years.
>
> Source: Interviews at Limerick Institute of Technology during the study visit in October 2015.

In October 2015, 900 students from all over Ireland received certificates, diplomas, higher diplomas, postgraduate diplomas and masters awards in a wide range of academic disciplines from ACE. Demonstrating to industry partners the value of knowledge and involving them in programme design are key success factors for ACE. For example, the higher diploma programme in Leadership Development has been taken up by senior managers from multinational corporations and large Irish firms. Recently, a programme for family business sustainability for SME owners and managers has been launched. In addition a range of community education programmes are offered at lower fee rates to facilitate participation. Some of the programmes are unique, for example, a programme in mental health in the community, and enrol students from all over Ireland. ACE also organises UCC's Springboard activities and, where possible, aims to integrate or link these courses into mainstream academic programmes.

Supporting entrepreneurship

The 2014 National Policy Statement on Entrepreneurship in Ireland (DJEI, 2014) assigns an essential role to the education and training system in re-enforcing positive perceptions of entrepreneurship and in fostering a culture that celebrates entrepreneurs and legitimises the entrepreneurial career path. This is further supported by the National Skills Strategy and its strong focus on entrepreneurship (DES, 2016).

At the HEI level entrepreneurship education is offered across the sector in various formats and across many disciplines. In all the HEIs visited and reviewed for this report there was clear evidence of the central role of students in the higher education system and the desire to help students develop entrepreneurial mindsets and behaviours. Course modules and programmes in entrepreneurship originated from the business schools within the HEIs and increasingly these have been adapted and transferred into other disciplines.

Fayolle (2013) reflected on some key educational and didactical issues around entrepreneurship education and concluded that it is too often perceived as a "factory producing startups", with an emphasis on functional dimensions and business-planning. A greater focus is needed on soft skills such as relational, conceptual, organising and commitment competencies in order to shift the approach towards developing (future) entrepreneurs, who are capable of thinking, acting and making decisions in a wide range of situations and contexts (Man et al., 2002). For this shift to happen, closer collaboration is needed between researchers and educators on methods in entrepreneurship education to embed the development of an entrepreneurial mindset and entrepreneurial thinking (Carsrud and Brännback, 2009), entrepreneurial action (Frese, 2009), entrepreneurial method (Sarasvathy and Venkataraman, 2011), effectuation and causation (Sarasvathy, 2001), and bricolage (Baker and Nelson, 2005).

In all HEIs visited and reviewed for this report, several excellent and promising activities are underway in this regard. Dedicated and professional entrepreneurship teams have introduced new initiatives and brought in international partners. Also, increasing efforts are directed towards capturing and measuring the impact of entrepreneurship education. Entrepreneurship education is fully backed by senior management. President's awards dedicated to entrepreneurship and innovation are effective initiatives to recognise and reward students and staff for their achievements and to motivate followers.

There is growing interest in entrepreneurship at all levels of study and several student societies and associations are actively promoting an entrepreneurial culture. Students interviewed, in general, felt that entrepreneurship was still heavily linked with business and commerce rather than with creativity and innovation. A wider understanding of entrepreneurship could be nurtured by campus-wide activities open to all undergraduate students. Entrepreneurs Anonymous at UCC is an example (Box 4.5). At some HEIs, there is a clear commitment from senior management to extend the concept of entrepreneurship and make it more relatable to students. The ENACTUS network at DCU has been pioneering this through a greater focus on social entrepreneurship.

Some of the entrepreneurship courses at undergraduate levels at the HEIs visited have more than 200 students. High levels of student intake may be useful to widely spread an overall interest in entrepreneurship; however, more opportunities to learn in smaller groups and interdisciplinary settings are needed for interested students to advance their projects, for example, by bringing together business and engineering students. There is great potential in Irish HEIs to spearhead developments in this direction, as suggested by the various efforts to incorporate the activities of the student societies and associations, who seek to expand engagement beyond business and marketing studies through hackathons and cross-campus initiatives.

The aim of building a cross-campus understanding that entrepreneurship is as much about processes and services, and not only about widgets and objects is very much alive at UL. Leading this is Design@UL, which connects a wide range of local, national and international partners and offers interdisciplinary education and creative learning spaces. Fourth-year design students collaborate in Real-World Studio Projects with companies on their innovation challenges. The aim is to design new products and business concepts. A "design manager", who is part of the UL teaching staff, facilitates the process. Students have "dummy" presentations in advance of going out to present to the companies. From second

> **Box 4.5. Entrepreneurs Anonymous at the University College of Cork**
>
> Students at the University College of Cork (UCC) have started the Entrepreneurs Anonymous initiative, which is not to be confused with the global initiative Entrepreneurship Anonymous. While the global initiative targets nascent entrepreneurs and those with a clear intention to start up a business, UCC's Entrepreneurs Anonymous takes a more encompassing and "low-key" approach. The overall aim is to encourage and facilitate exchange and discussion of ideas, which could lead to entrepreneurial activities in the broadest sense.
>
> Entrepreneurs Anonymous is a creative space for like-minded people to explore entrepreneurship. Members organise get-togethers and wider networking events to share experiences and ideas. An example is the "Unpitch" sessions where students and other interested people get the chance to present an entrepreneurial idea in a casual and no-pressure environment. Presentations last five minutes followed by five minutes for Q&A. These sessions are more brainstorming sessions amongst peers than a pitch presentation to potential investors or customers.
>
> The friendly and supportive environment helps students to build self-confidence, presentation skills, and learn the difference between assertive and reflective assessments. Entrepreneurs Anonymous at UCC is present on various social networks.
>
> *Source:* Interviews at University College of Cork during the study visit in October 2015.

year onwards, students build up to this level of interaction by working on their soft skills. Current partner firms include multinational corporations, large firms and local start-ups.

DICE (Digital Innovation, Creativity and Enterprise) is a first-year module at DCU which has been offered since 2012 and has involved over 350 first-year and nearly 200 postgraduate students annually from the faculties of business and computing. Students are taught through team work, live webinars, project work and mini-conferences with speakers and attendees from the wider business community. Students start by identifying what types of learning work for them. Synchronous online learning is enhanced by creating websites and blogs, for example on WordPress, and with the completion of a personal blog at each of the mini-conferences. A structured research programme runs alongside this (Box 4.6). This type of activity could be offered to all students.

> **Box 4.6. Digital Innovation, Creativity and Enterprise at Dublin City University**
>
> The Dublin City University (DCU) has developed a first-year module, Digital Innovation, Creativity and Enterprise (DICE), to enhance students' digital technology skills as well as teaching entrepreneurial skills. The aim of DICE is to expose students to industry and different modes of learning as early as possible. DICE seeks to develop students' skills in key areas in order to prepare them for the reality of the business world. In particular, within the DICE module, students are encouraged to identify what types of learning work for them. DICE students have access to blended learning (e.g. on WordPress or PRINCE2 Project Management), live webinars, peer-learning during project work and mini-conferences with speakers from the business community.
>
> The mini-conferences deal with topics such as using mobile marketing, cloud computing and social media for venture (start-up) activities. Students keep a personal blog on each of the mini-conferences and are encouraged to self-reflect on the learning outcomes of those

> **Box 4.6. Digital Innovation, Creativity and Enterprise at Dublin City University** *(cont.)*
>
> conferences and on other activities. DICE students also participate in the development of a mobile app in a cross-faculty team utilising cloud computing technology. This is supervised by postgraduate students, who have completed the Next Generation Management module.
>
> The Next Generation Management is a module available to Masters students at DCU. The aim is to develop meta-cognitive skills that allow students to become innovative, critical thinkers as well as adaptive, flexible and pro-active in the management of projects. Four pillars guide this process: raising awareness for global and societal issues, training in digital media communication, and personal as well as career development. Students work on a "reflective portfolio", which contains a personal development plan and a description of personal opportunities for development.
>
> *Source:* Interviews at Dublin City University during the study visit in October 2015.

UCC has created a cohesive approach to entrepreneurship for postgraduate level programmes. Central to this is IGNITE, a one-year programme, which offers a wide range of support for students to start their own businesses. IGNITE lasts nine months and offers participants a scholarship of EUR 5 000, technical seminars and networking events, access to a "hot desk", which is a work space with information and communications technology facilities, and one-on-one business mentoring from leading entrepreneurs in Cork, as well as support from "Coaches on Campus", which are academic staff that offer coaching and mentoring. Technology intensive ideas can, for example, be developed during a placement in one of the research centres at UCC.

Spreading entrepreneurship education across campus

Academic staff at Dundalk Institute of Technology (DkIT) recognised, in the academic year 2012/13, the need to systematise the desired change in mindsets and entrepreneurial behaviours, and started a formal programme to embed specific competence modules in all programmes. The academic Council was supportive and a programmatic review exercise was started in each of DkIT's four schools to make sure that all programmes contain some element of entrepreneurship. To support this, the all-campus Entrepreneurship Enterprise Working Group was established under the Academic Council. Its activities have moved from general promotion of its objectives of encouraging cross-HEI academic developments in entrepreneurship education to an audit-type role ensuring course development and review includes entrepreneurship learning opportunities.

Another example of spreading entrepreneurship education across campus is the "Market-Link Entrepreneur" programme at LIT, which is offered to students from all faculties. The programme is designed to encourage students to develop business ideas, and involves a series of business workshops. There has been a noticeable increase in the number of students from all departments in recent years coming forward with business ideas.

The Quercus Talented Students Scholarship at UCC celebrates extraordinary talent and links UCC with families, second-level schools and other local stakeholders. One of the award categories is entrepreneurship and innovation; others are academic and sporting achievement, active citizenship and the creative and performing arts. Applications for the awards can come from prospective undergraduate students and current UCC students.

Successful applicants receive a year-long and renewable scholarship worth up to EUR 10 000 per annum. Quercus entrepreneurship and innovation scholars are expected to act as Idea-Ambassadors who widely spread the entrepreneurial mindset and culture.

Another notable initiative is the Blackstone LaunchPad at UCC. In collaboration with the Blackstone Foundation, which is based in the US, a shared learning space is under construction in the library building with grid spaces and whiteboards for creativity exercises and presentations. The aim is to offer maximum access to students, ideally 24/7. This will also involve a repurposing of the entire building for which UCC has committed resources. It will also be important to fully integrate the facility into UCC's structures, including staffing arrangements, which will include both UCC and Blackstone employees.

Strengthening local entrepreneurship ecosystems

The presence of multiple HEIs in close proximity or even within the same city provides an excellent opportunity to build local ecosystems for entrepreneurship. The system performance framework could build on this and encourage HEIs to increase activity and collaboration in this area. This could be supported by targeted funding,

An example that offers relevant learnings is the 4Entrepreneurship initiative in the city of Munich (Box 4.7).

Box 4.7. The "4Entrepreneurship" in Munich

The Technical University of Munich, the Ludwig Maximilian's University of Munich, the University of the Federal Armed Forces, and the Munich University of Applied Sciences are collaborating in the "4Entrepreneurship" network, which provides various opportunities for students and staff of the four HEIs to take part in entrepreneurial activities at all the institutions in the network.

In 2010, the Social Entrepreneurship Akademie (SEA) was established as a joint initiative by the four university-based entrepreneurship centres in Munich as part of "4Entrepreneurship". SEA is used to stimulate entrepreneurial thinking across all university disciplines. SEA positions social impact as a strategic decision for organisations [www.seakademie.de]. Under the slogan "Education for societal change" this network organisation educates social entrepreneurs or social change-makers. Founding members and partners include the four universities plus 10 strategic partners: the BMW Foundation, Herbert Quandt, Bonventure, Vodafone Foundation Germany, Stifterverband für die Deutsche Wissenschaft, HypoVereinbank, Telefonica, kfw-Foundation, Bertelsmann Foundation, Hans Sauer Foundation, Siemens Foundation, and Unicredit Foundation. In 2013 SEA had more than 220 000 likes on Facebook and established over 15 international partnerships with similar initiatives.

The potential to systematically organise knowledge exchange and resource pooling was tested in 2013. FutureLAB of Architecture started a 3D house printing initiative with students from the University of California, Los Angeles; the University of Huddersfield in the UK; Tokyo University and Chiba University, Japan; the Technical University of Munich and the MUAS. After 60 hours of 3D printing, the first printed house was ready for around EUR 60 000 [www.futurelabstudio.org].

The "4Entrepreneurship" hosted the "Global Venture Summit" in Munich in 2016, a global outreach event for start-ups, innovators and top-investors from all over the world.

Source: HEInnovate (2017b).

Conclusions

Stimulating innovation and entrepreneurship through education plays an important role in Irish higher education and entrepreneurship education is offered across the sector in various formats and across many disciplines. In all the HEIs visited and reviewed for this report there was clear evidence of the central role of students in the higher education system and the desire to help students develop entrepreneurial mindsets and behaviours.

Course modules and programmes in entrepreneurship originated from the business schools within the HEIs. Increasingly these have been adapted and transferred into other disciplines and in some cases adopted across a multiple of disciplines within HEIs. Efforts should be increased to organise education activities on creativity, innovation and entrepreneurship, which involve students from different faculties and departments in the form of (optional) interdisciplinary modules throughout the duration of their studies. These activities develop "soft" skills which enable students to communicate in entrepreneurial terms outside of their traditional disciplinary silos and make graduates so valuable to employers. They should be embedded into the curriculum, rather than organised as "add-ons".

The organisation of interdisciplinary idea generation workshops, which bring together researchers, students and knowledge users can be a good starting point for more collaboration across disciplines. To engage staff, a specific award could be introduced for interdisciplinary achievements, such as the development and application of conceptualisations, theories, sources and methods that are drawn from different disciplines in order to define and resolve problems in novel ways. It will be important to link these activities with the case studies on (research) impact. In this regard, training for staff and students will be important to develop impact awareness.

Notes

1. Luxemburg has, with 66% tertiary attainment in the age group 30-34 years, the highest target amongst the EU-28 countries; Italy has, with 26%, the lowest target (EUROSTAT).
2. REAP was led by Cork Institute of Technology and involved as partners Athlone Institute of Technology, Dublin Institute of Technology, Sligo Institute of Technology, Tallaght Institute of Technology, the National University of Ireland, Galway, the University College Cork and Waterford Institute of Technology. See *http://arrow.dit.ie*. for a rich repository of project findings, guidelines and case studies.

References

Armbruster, C. (2008), "Research universities: Autonomy and self-reliance after the entrepreneurial university", *Policy Futures in Education*, 6(4), 372-389.

Baker, T. and R.E. Nelson (2005), "Creating something from nothing: Resource construction through entrepreneurial bricolage", *Administrative Science Quarterly* 50 (3), 329-366.

Boudon, R. (1974), *Education, Opportunity, and Social Inequality: Changing Prospects in Western Society*, Wiley-Interscience, New York.

Bouter, L.M. (2008), "Knowledge as public property: The societal relevance of scientific research", *OECD's Higher Education Management and Policy Journal*, www.oecd.org/site/eduimhe08/41203349.pdf (accessed 11 February 2017).

Carsrud, A. and M. Brännback (2009), *Understanding the Entrepreneurial Mind*, Springer, New York.

Department of Education and Skills (2011), *National Strategy for Higher Education to 2030*, published online, www.hea.ie/sites/default/files/national_strategy_for_higher_education_2030.pdf (accessed 11 February 2017).

Department of Education and Skills (2015), *Country Background Report Ireland*, prepared for the HEInnovate Ireland country review, unpublished report submitted to the OECD.

Department for Education and Skills (2016), *National Skills Strategy 2025 – Ireland's Future*, published online, *www.education.ie/en/Publications/Policy-Reports/pub_national_skills_strategy_2025.pdf* (accessed 11 February 2017).

Department of Enterprise, Jobs and Innovation (2013), *Addressing Future Demand for High-Level ICT Skills*, Dublin.

Department of Enterprise, Jobs and Innovation (2014), *National Policy Statement on Entrepreneurship in Ireland*, published online, *www.localenterprise.ie/Documents-and-Publications/Entrepreneurship-in-Ireland-2014.pdf* (accessed 11 February 2017).

ESRI (2013), *A Study of Future Demand for Higher Education in Ireland*, Dublin.

EUROSTAT (2016), "Tertiary educational attainment by sex, age group 30-34", *http://ec.europa.eu/eurostat/tgm/table.do?tab=table&init=1&plugin=1&language=en&pcode=t2020_41* (accessed 30 March 2016).

Expert Group on Future Skills Needs (2012), *Addressing Future Demand for High-Level ICT Skills*, published online, *www.skillsireland.ie/media/04112013-Addressing_ICT_Skills-Publication.pdf* (accessed 11 February 2017).

Fayolle, A. (2013), Personal views on the future of entrepreneurship education, *Entrepreneurship & Regional Development: An International Journal*, 25:7-8, 692-701, *http://dx.doi.org/10.1080/08985626.2013.821318*.

Frese, M. (2009), "Toward a Psychology of Entrepreneurship – An Action Theory Perspective", *Foundations and Trends in Entrepreneurship* 5:6, 437-496.

HEInnovate (2017a), "Internationalisation at Aalborg University", published online, *https://heinnovate.eu/resource/internationalisation-aalborg-university* (accessed 14 February 2017).

HEInnovate (2017b), "Strascheg Center for Entrepreneurship at the University of Applied Sciences Munich", published online, *https://heinnovate.eu/resource/strascheg-center-entrepreneurship-university-applied-sciences-munich* (accessed 14 February 2017).

Higher Education Authority, SOLAS, Quality and Qualifications Ireland, Department for Education and Skills (2015), *National Employer Survey*, published online, *www.qqi.ie/Downloads/EmployerSurveyMay 2015final.pdf#search=Employer%20survey%20** (accessed 11 February 2017).

Irish Universities Association and Irish Research Council (2016), *Engaged Research. Addressing Grand Societal Challenges Together*, published online, *www.campusengage.ie/sites/default/files/FINAL%20JAN%2016_ER%20Report%202016%20Jan%20v2.pdf* (accessed 11 February 2017).

Man, T.W.Y., T. Lau and K.F. Chan (2002), "The competitiveness of small and medium enterprises: A conceptualisation with focus on entrepreneurial competencies", *Journal of Business Venturing* 17 (2): 123-142.

OECD (2006), *Think Scenarios, Rethink Education*, OECD Publishing, Paris.

Sarasvathy, S. (2001), "Causation and effectuation: A theoretical shift from economic inevitability to entrepreneurial contingency", *Academy of Management Review*, 28 (2): 243-263.

Sarasvathy, S.D. and S. Venkataraman (2011), "Entrepreneurship as a method: Open questions for an entrepreneurial future", *Entrepreneurship Theory and Practice*, 35, 1: 113-135.

Sheridan, I. and M. Linehan (2011), *Work Placement in Third-Level Programmes in Ireland*, published online, *http://arrow.dit.ie/cgi/viewcontent.cgi?article=1005&context=reaprepo*.

Chapter 5

Enhancing the impact of Ireland's higher education institutions

This chapter expands on the findings presented in Chapter 2 with a focus on the impact of higher education and the possible results of a greater emphasis on entrepreneurship and innovation. There are significant opportunities for HEIs to have positive impacts on their local economies, not only directly but in a wide range of indirect ways, both on the supply and demand side. However, as discussed in this chapter, there are also a range of tensions that need to be understood and carefully managed by the HEIs themselves, their local partners and national policy makers if impacts are to be effectively delivered.

Introduction

Higher education institutions (HEIs) played a critical role in the development of Ireland's economy and the sector is recognised by policy makers as a key factor in driving the post-crash recovery, in particular its ability to attract foreign direct investment and enhance growth of Irish businesses.

It has been the strategy of successive governments since the late 1960s to increase participation in higher education from what were historically low levels in comparison with other "developed" economies. This has resulted in Ireland currently having the highest proportion of 30-34 year olds with higher education qualifications in Europe, one of the factors highlighted by many commentators (e.g. Gunnigle and McGuire, 2001) in Ireland's success in attracting foreign direct investment during the so-called "Celtic Tiger" period from the mid-1990s to the mid-2000s.

These high participation rates combined with a still growing young population mean that the number of people participating in higher education is expected to grow by nearly 30% over the next 15 years, from a current base of 215 000. However this growth in student numbers is taking place in the context of reduced government funding for higher education. Between 2007/08 and 2015/16 the recurrent government expenditure for higher education fell from EUR 1.85 billion to EUR 1.7 billion, a reduction of 8%. When coupled with a growing student population this actually represents a fall of 24% in real terms of funding per student during the same period (DES, 2015). However, this trend is now being reversed with an increase in the higher education budget in 2017 and the publication of a recent expert group report which provides recommendations for consideration on the creation of a sustainable funding model for higher education (HEA, 2016a).

Analysis and findings

In these circumstances, how can Irish HEIs maximise their impact on social and economic development? This can be explored by looking at the ways in which HEIs contribute to development and growth, what tensions and challenges they face in delivering impact and how these might be managed or overcome.

Irish HEIs as "anchor" institutions

The Work Foundation defines anchor institutions as:

"Large locally embedded institutions, typically non-governmental public sector, cultural or other civic institutions that are of significant importance to the economy and the wider community life of the cities in which they are based. They generate positive externalities and relationships that can support or "anchor" wider economic activity in the locality.... Their scale, local rootedness and community links are such that they can play a key role in local development and economic growth representing the "sticky capital" around which economic growth strategies can be built". (Work Foundation, 2010)

In the case of HEIs their main location, in comparison with private firms, is fixed within the current home location. Notwithstanding possible expansion to other nearby or far away campuses it is where they have considerable sunk investment in buildings and strong identification with place, not least through the name of the institution. On past experience HEIs have generally been immune to institutional failure or sudden contractions in size. They can therefore act as a source of stability in local economies, buffering against the worst effects of periodic downturns. They are particularly important as anchor institutions in weaker economies (Goddard et al., 2014).

The importance of this anchoring role in Irish HEIs is even more pronounced due to the highly centralised nature of Ireland and its economy. Dublin accounts for around 25% of the national population; almost 40% live in the greater Dublin area. These population ratios are projected to remain the same to 2031, with the Greater Dublin Area region seeing a small increase of 3.1%, and other regions declining somewhat. 42% of Ireland's gross domestic product (GDP) is accounted for by Dublin. In comparison, London accounts for 20% of the UK's GDP (WDC, 2014). Compared to other European countries, Ireland's "second tier" cities are dwarfed by the capital. Cork City with a population of just under 120 000 is the only other Irish city with a population of more than 100 000 (CSO, 2011).

With the population and economic activity highly concentrated around the capital it is not surprising that Dublin and its wider area constitute the most institutionally "thick" part of the country in terms of research and innovation. Four of the country's seven universities are located in or close to Dublin and more than half of other public research organisations (SFI, 2016) are based in the capital. The concentration of HEIs and other research institutes around Dublin can result in a mutually reinforcing effect of funding success leading to improved capacity. The fact that over 55% of total funding to Irish HEIs from the European Union's Seventh Framework Programme for Research and Technological Development (FP7), and 34% of all FP7 funds went to HEIs in Dublin is evidence of this (European Commission, 2014).

This means that HEIs outside the capital are vitally important to their local innovation ecosystems, and in many cases (especially in non-metropolitan places) they may be "the only game in town" in terms of research. In particular the IOTs are critically important to their local economies, especially outside the four "core" cities where they are the sole local HEI provider. In an era of reduced funding and increased competition the danger is that innovation "cold spots" are reinforced or emerge outside the capital. Supporting HEIs to develop their research capacity and connect to local businesses can create significant, and disproportionately positive, impacts for the local and national economy.

The IOTs are under significant pressure. Key factors are high teaching loads and less flexibility in recruitment, which further limits their capacity to acquire competitive funding. IOTs are subject to the same recruitment conditions as universities, but they are more restricted in terms of being able to borrow money to invest. There is no capacity to make people redundant where courses are no longer relevant. This has impacted IOTs, particularly when the construction sector collapsed along with participation in apprenticeships in relevant trades.

Direct economic impact

It is an uncontested fact that HEIs have a significant direct impact on their local economy (Henderson, 2001). They are significant employers, procurers of services and a catalyst for new enterprise activity. HEIs attract students and skilled staff from outside the region, who stimulate economic activity through their spending on housing and other local goods and services. A number of studies have looked at the economic impact of the sector as a whole (Zhang et al, 2015) as well as individual institutions (Biggar Economics, 2013; DCU, 2015). These have reinforced the contention that spending on higher education has a significant multiplier effect on the local and national economy.[1]

Employment in HEIs in Ireland accounted for around 1.2% of total employment in 2010-11 (Zhang et al, 2015). This compares with a figure of 1.3% in the United Kingdom in 2013 according to HESA, a charitable company operating under a statutory framework on behalf of the funding councils and government departments. In terms of overall economic impact the outputs of Irish HEIs have a more significant effect, accounting for 5.5% of national GDP in 2010-11. This is almost double the proportion of GDP accounted for by the sector in the United Kingdom; 2.8% in 2011-12 (Zhang et al., 2015). HEIs in Ireland account for a disproportionately high level of economic output relative to the size of the sector, and are more significant in terms of their impact compared to other countries. Following this logic, reductions in funding for higher education could have a far greater impact on the economy than the value of the "real terms" reduction.

Investing more in higher education would provide a significant stimulus to the economy. This is being facilitated by current efforts to identify new funding sources and the prioritisation of new funding models already underway (HEA, 2016a).

Research and innovation

As already shown, Irish HEIs are key anchor institutions in the national and local innovation systems, especially in innovation "thin" places outside the capital. The success of Irish HEIs in attracting funds, such as FP7, shows their importance as catalysts in unlocking collaborative research funding both nationally and internationally which smaller organisations, especially small and medium-sized enterprises (SMEs) may not have the capacity or networks to pursue alone.

Research centres are an excellent tool for building collaborations between HEIs, other research institutions and the private sector in line with thematic areas of the research prioritisation exercise which lends coherence and alignment with national strategies. Science Foundation Ireland (SFI) has established twelve research centres in Ireland to create partnerships across academia and industry to address crucial research questions; foster the development of new and existing Irish-based technology companies; attract industry that could make an important contribution to Ireland and its economy; and expand educational and career opportunities in Ireland in science and engineering. Investment to establish the centres included EUR 355 million from public sources and a further EUR 190 million from industry. The SFI Research Centres have been very active in terms of spin-off activities, licensing and other forms of technology transfer activities. They closely collaborate with the Technology Centres of Enterprise Ireland.

Research activities in HEIs, especially when aggregated into well-defined and resourced hubs and centres can also act as a magnet to attract additional private investment in research and development activities. For example, the decision by Johnson and Johnson to open their new information technology services centre on the UL campus was in part driven by the presence of Lero, the Irish Software Engineering Research Centre, and the expertise in UL's Computer Science and Information Systems Department.

Irish HEIs depend on a range of state and semi-state bodies and European sources for the bulk of their research funding. All of these are allocated competitively and have their own, often complex processes for application and reporting. Funding pressures (especially but not only in the IOTs) have meant that there is limited capacity to keep up with the various systems and processes in order to respond to calls and to "invest" the time and effort needed to develop proposals of a sufficient quality (see also Chapter 3).

There is a need to demonstrate the value of the research being carried out by the academics within the HEIs as part of their work that is not funded by research funders. Ireland's research citations are 16th in global scientific ranking and, for example, first in Nanoscience and second in Immunology, but from a system-perspective there is no performance measurement. While there are numerous sources of information on various *activities*, these are not being translated effectively (enough) into details of their actual *impacts* in terms of the economy and society at large.

Core funding for research could be allocated on the basis of quality and impact of existing research in the HEIs. This would show the value of the block grant to the research system. Further, mechanisms could be put in place to provide researchers with more capacity (either for themselves or through provision of support) to seek and apply for research opportunities. National funding programmes could be further consolidated, simplified and common processes put in place.

In research funding it has been shown that success breeds success (University Alliance, 2009). There is a danger of a widening gap between the *best* Irish performers in attracting research funding and the *rest*, as the more successful institutions have more resources to invest in attracting staff, equipment and further funding. There is also a geographic element to this as Dublin (and other larger cities) are attracting a disproportionate amount of funding which could result in research and innovation "cold spots" emerging or being reinforced in other parts of the country. Enterprise Ireland had, until recently, only set national targets; a more-regional/local approach will help HEIs to build and sustain their local development role not only in the graduates they produce but also through their job creation, R&D, business incubation and community development initiatives.

The Irish Research Council (IRC) has launched its Making an Impact Competition as part of the "#loveIrishresearch" campaign, which is an initiative aimed at highlighting the achievements of Irish researchers and the effective communication of their work to a lay audience. With a prize fund of EUR 5 000 it is an opportunity for students registered in postgraduate programmes across all disciplines to share their research. Two awards are offered with EUR 2 500 each, one decided by the panel and the other based on an audience vote. Winning research will be profiled by the Irish Independent. Unsuccessful finalists will receive a EUR 100 book voucher. Since its launch in 2009, the initiative has attracted a huge variety of submissions. Winning entries in 2015 were on topics as diverse as ultra-high-performance reinforced concrete and the role of omega-3 from algae in gut and brain health (HEA, 2016b).

The University of Limerick offers an excellent example of how to describe research impact through the use of case studies (Box 5.1). The initiative was started by the Vice-President for Research who brought together groups of researchers from different faculties and worked with them in order to develop an understanding of "what" impact is and "how" it can be measured (see also Chapter 4).

The role of all disciplines, in particular areas other than Science, Technology, Engineering and Mathematics (STEM), in delivering social innovation and addressing societal challenges needs to be further highlighted and reflected in national funding

> **Box 5.1. Impact Case Studies at the University of Limerick**
>
> How do we ensure our government and its policies are informed by the needs of our citizens? How do we encourage our citizens to become active participants in forming the policies which affect their future? These are questions which researchers at the University of Limerick (UL) seek to answer.
>
> Dr Maura Adshead together with Dr Chris McInerney of the Department of Politics and Public Administration, University of Limerick have led the development of innovative practice in the area of policy research and civic engagement. Dr Adshead explains: "Best practice suggests that all policy should be evidence based but policy-makers rarely have access to those whom policy most affects. With the exception of a few focus groups or opinion polls, it is often hard for policy makers and politicians to know what really works "on the ground". Our research finds ways to enable ordinary people to express their opinions and influence policy formulation and implementation more effectively".
>
> Their research has made an impact on public policy and planning projects such as the Clare Immigrant Strategy and the Ennis 2020 Community Visioning and Participatory Planning Initiative. In the Ennis 2020 initiative the UL research team developed a process that would enable deeper engagement between residents of the town and its council to imaging a vision of the community's future.
>
> Dr McInerney added; "Our research has shown us that a policy of ensuring the voice of the people is heard leads to greater citizen engagement, and ultimately strong civic pride and better communities. The Ennis 2020 project is an excellent example of research policy and practice being applied and leading to greater citizen to Council engagement and ultimately building towards a better future". The work on Ennis 2020 has informed the training of public administration officials at a national and local level and has been applied in a number of communities including migrants and asylum seekers.
>
> Source: University of Limerick (2016).

priorities. Case studies such as NetwellCASALA in Dundalk could be further developed to showcase the importance of transdisciplinary research.

Universities and research funders could explore the use of innovative tools like sandpits to bring together researchers in different disciplines in order to build collaborative projects and proposals (Box 5.2). This has been practiced since 2004 by the Engineering and Physical Sciences Research Council (EPSRC), the main government agency for funding research and training in engineering and the physical sciences in the United Kingdom. The EPSRC invests around GBP 740 million per annum in universities in a broad range of STEM subjects. The sandpits are part of the IDEAS Factory concept. Participants are selected for each sandpit according to their skills and expertise. Sandpits often have a rich diversity bringing together physical scientists, engineers, designers, social scientists, psychologists and healthcare specialists (EPRSC, n.d.).

Enterprise and entrepreneurship

Irish HEIs help to promote enterprise[2] and entrepreneurship in a number of ways. They support spin-offs and start-ups from staff, students and alumni. They help develop entrepreneurial skills amongst students through societies, competitions and prizes, teaching and learning, project based learning, work placements etc. HEIs are also involved more broadly in local and regional activities to promote and support entrepreneurship, for

> **Box 5.2. Sandpits to build transdisciplinary projects and proposals**
>
> Sandpits are residential interactive workshops over five days. They have a highly multidisciplinary mix of 20-30 participants, some active researchers and others potential users of research outcomes, to drive lateral thinking and radical approaches to address research challenges. Sandpits are intensive discussion forums where free thinking is encouraged to delve into the problems on the agenda to uncover innovative solutions.
>
> The Engineering and Physical Sciences Research Council (EPSRC) in the United Kingdom has been working with sandpits since 2004 as part of their IDEAS Factory. Sandpits often have a rich diversity bringing together physical scientists, engineers, designers, social scientists, psychologists and healthcare specialists. Each sandpit is led by a director, who defines the topic and facilitates discussions at the event. A group of stakeholders and subject experts facilitate the process as mentors. This group is not eligible to receive research funding so acts as an impartial referee in the process.
>
> The process can be broken down into five output-driven phases:
>
> 1. Defining the scope of the issue
> 2. Agreeing a common language and terminology amongst diverse backgrounds and disciplines
> 3. Sharing various perspectives on the issue
> 4. Using creative and innovative thinking techniques in break-out sessions to focus on a problem
> 5. Turning Sandpit outputs into a research project
>
> Sandpits are intensive events and for the well-being of participants, venues offer relaxation opportunities, and the timetable includes informal networking activities as a break from detailed technical discussions. Due to group dynamics and continual evaluation it is not possible to "dip in and out" of the process. Participants must stay for the whole duration of the event.
>
> Sandpit funding is not spread evenly across participants: a variety of outcomes are possible, ranging from a single large research project, to several smaller projects, feasibility studies, networking activities, overseas visits and so on. Outcomes are not pre-determined, but are defined during the sandpit.
>
> *Source:* (EPRSC, n.d.).

example the annual Start-up Gathering events. Another example is the Student Enterprise Awards at Galway Mayo Institute of Technology (Box 5.3).

While all HEIs offer entrepreneurship education to a lesser or greater extent, this is not always available to every student or formalised within their curriculum (e.g. in terms of course credits etc.). In some cases, enterprise is still perceived as a topic focused on or restricted to students of business and commerce. However there are a number of challenges in embedding enterprise education, especially if students are to work together across disciplines, in terms of resources and timetabling (see Chapter 4).

Alumni networks could be more effectively built and deployed to identify growth potential businesses, and also to act as mentors. Entrepreneurial education and training could be offered to all students in more formalised and accredited ways. Giving students opportunities to work on projects that cut across disciplines can spark innovative business ideas as well as developing future workplace skills for team working.

> Box 5.3. **Students Enterprise Awards at Galway Mayo Institute of Technology**
>
> The competition is run in all five campuses across the Galway Mayo Institute of Technology (GMIT). All finalists are assigned a GMIT mentor to help prepare them for GMIT Students Enterprise Awards Final, which will be a ten-minute pitching competition to an external panel.
>
> First place winner receives a cash prize of EUR 2 000 plus free hot desking space for 3 months in the GMIT Innovation Hubs (Mayo or Galway) plus mentoring support. Second place receives a cash prize of EUR 500 plus free hot desking space for 3 months in the GMIT Innovation Hubs (Mayo or Galway). Third place receives a cash prize of EUR 300. Fourth place receives a cash prize of EUR 200.
>
> Source: Interviews at Galway Mayo Institute of Technology during the study visit in October 2015.

Therefore should (or to what extent could) they align their entrepreneurship support activities to the needs of the local economy? Should support be directed towards those businesses that will fill gaps locally, or complement existing industrial activity? Or should enterprise support for students and graduates be focused on the needs and ambitions of the individuals involved, regardless of local need? Where the focus is on supporting individuals, there may be a danger that new activity merely displaces existing businesses, and there is no net gain to the local economy. However being overly prescriptive in which businesses will be selected or rejected for support may discourage some from pursuing their ideas.

As with all forms of business support, there are critical questions around sustainability and additionality. Is support enabling businesses to survive that would not succeed alone? And if businesses should be expected to succeed without support, to what extent can it be seen to deliver added value (for example, faster growth)? These are difficult issues which have been extensively studied and researched by the What Works Centre for Local Economic Growth (2014) without any conclusive findings, but still need to be considered when designing enterprise and business support programmes.

Many of the start-up support programmes run by Irish HEIs are financed by the Department of Jobs, Enterprise, and Innovation (DJEI) and delivered through Enterprise Ireland. The key objective of these programmes is to achieve specific national targets, e.g. number of businesses started, job creation, export sales etc. Focusing on outputs, particularly where they need to be achieved in a relatively short timeframe could result in driving behaviour towards a tendency to back "sure things" rather than more high risk (but high potential) propositions.

There could be a more joined up approach with local enterprise agencies to ensure a seamless offer for new businesses in order to ensure continuity, lack of duplication and co-ordination in terms of funding, support and accommodation etc.

Human capital and skills development

Impact on human capital and skills development is obviously at the heart of the role of HEIs. The Irish higher education system has been particularly successful in building the skills profile of the population from what were historically low levels to one of the highest levels of participation in the developed world. In the mid-1960s just 2% of school leavers entered higher education. In recent years more than half of school leavers have progressed to graduate level programmes.

As with most countries, participation in higher education in Ireland is strongly correlated with the education level of parents. Members of the travelling community are particularly under-represented. In common with many other countries, people with mental and physical disabilities, and people from deprived communities are also less likely to progress to higher education. Here, several policy initiatives have been introduced to increase access to and progression in higher education.

The binary system of higher education has been critical in creating a bridge into higher education amongst non-traditional learners and therefore the IOTs are a crucial element in maintaining increasing participation rates and especially amongst under-represented groups by offering "stepping stones" towards Level 8 upwards qualifications. For example, 80% of students at DKIT are first generation higher education learners. Almost 50% more students at LIT qualify for the student maintenance grant compared to the national average. LIT also has double the average number of students with a disability at 9%. The proximity of HEIs to large communities with a history of economic and social deprivation has clearly been an important factor in promoting the visibility (and possibility) of higher education to non-traditional participants (see Chapter 4). In the visited IOTs teaching loads and staff-student ratios are close to (or even beyond) acceptable limits. With the number of students expected to grow for another ten years this position will not be sustainable.

In terms of investment in education, the focus of politicians and the public at large is on primary and second-level education, which are also under enormous pressure from increasing numbers and reduced funding. In this context, it is difficult to argue for prioritisation and funding for higher education which is not seen as a fundamental right in the same way primary and second-level education is.

Another issue that seems to particularly pertain to Ireland is lack of student mobility. Irish students traditionally do not travel long distances for their higher education. Of students living in counties with an HEI, the majority (around 80%) are enrolled at an HEI in their home county, based on data gathered by the Higher Education Authority (HEA) on county of residence of enrolled students at HEA funded institutions 2014/15. By way of comparison, less than 50% of English students stay in their home region to study, despite there being multiple institutions and much larger geographies concerned. The high concentration of HEIs in and around Dublin gives people much more choice. There needs to be a change in culture of students travelling to study and of HEIs becoming more specialised and focused. There are a number of reasons behind these low levels of mobility, ranging from cultural norms to financial constraints to housing shortages. However the sector should consider the implications of these relatively low levels of mobility.

Firstly, it means that students in higher education "cold spots", where there are no HEIs in commuting distance are potentially disadvantaged in terms of choice compared to students in the major cities and their surrounding areas, all of which have at least two HEIs. Dublin alone has three universities (plus Maynooth University within less than 30 km), four IOTs, as well as numerous other colleges and specialist (including private) institutions. This results in pressure being brought to bear on and by politicians for universities to be established in areas perceived to be higher education cold spots.

Secondly, it may constrain choice, hamper specialisation and risk duplication as students may be going to the nearest place rather than the best place to study their chosen topic (HEA, 2013). If students won't travel to specific institutions for specific courses then local institutions (especially where they are the sole provider in the area) are under pressure to provide a "full menu" of subjects.

In terms of the role of HEIs contributing to the human capital of the country, it has been suggested that many of the "best" (i.e. highest achievers at second-level) Irish students go overseas to study at more internationally prestigious universities. A significant number of these will not return to work in Ireland, especially those who have left for postgraduate studies.

Many HEIs highlight the insufficient/inadequate careers advice in schools at second-level and lack of knowledge amongst parents about opportunities and career paths (especially in STEM industries) as another challenge in ensuring Irish students are studying the subjects at third level that will deliver the skills needed to supply the demand for human capital in Ireland's growth sectors. While there is already evidence of links to local schools and communities via outreach and access programmes etc., more could be done in a more systemised way. Supporting careers advisors to understand the range of opportunities that new industries offer is key to ensuring students make informed choices later on. This support needs to happen before the final senior cycle when subject choices for the Leaving Certificate have already been made. Ideally, HEIs should be engaging with schools, pupils and parents at the end of primary and early years of second-level school.

Regional initiatives, such as Regional Clusters and Regional Skills Fora, if well organised, supported by the HEIs and properly resourced, can be an important method to achieving more co-operation between providers, increased pathways into and between HEIs, and building better links with further education providers and schools.

HEIs also play an important role in lifelong learning, continuous professional development, workforce development etc. IOTs in particular have higher numbers of mature[3] full and part-time students than average (16% compared to 8% in universities). The economic crisis has led to the development of some very innovative approaches to support unemployed people to reskill in new sectors where there is higher demand. Developing skills/reskilling amongst mature learners is a key factor in driving up the human capital in Ireland to a level needed for economic recovery and success. There is clear evidence of success in initiatives like the Springboard Programme. Promoting higher education for mature learners has wider benefits as feedback from the interviewed staff in HEIs would suggest that the presence of mature students helps other learners and drives up quality because of the prior knowledge and high expectations they bring to their learning experience (see Chapter 4).

Further innovation in teaching and programme delivery should be encouraged. There are many examples of HEIs teaching through project-based learning, blended learning, placements, co-operative models etc. There is also potential for tools such as electronic diaries to be developed further and mainstreamed.

Social and cultural development

HEIs can play a significant role in the social and cultural development of their local areas. IOTs in particular have been very instrumental in promoting social mobility, evidenced by higher than average levels of students on maintenance grants, from disadvantaged backgrounds, with disabilities and mature students. Feedback from students suggests that IOTs are seen as more locally oriented and accessible (smaller class sizes and classroom based learning makes for an easier transition from school compared to traditional universities).

Irish HEIs in general are often home to or sponsors of sports, art, music, museum and theatre facilities which are accessible to the public. They can also be instrumental in developing capacity locally for arts and culture, for example the University of Limerick and Limerick Institute of Technology are playing a pivotal role in the bid for Limerick to become European Capital of Culture in 2020. Shared facilities, joint ownership, establishing community interest companies and social enterprise etc. are effective models that HEIs and local communities can explore to ensure the sustainability of local sports, arts and cultural facilities.

In addition to the above-mentioned pressures on the core teaching and research budgets, recent years have also seen significant funding cuts for adult education and community and cultural/arts projects (e.g. Dorrity, 2010; Irish Congress of Trade Unions Community Sector Committee, 2012). This will have an impact on the ability of HEIs to contribute directly to the social and cultural development of their local areas, and will have deeper impacts in more peripheral places where there may be few if any alternative providers. At the same time local communities and authorities have high expectations of the role HEIs could/should play in social and cultural development. These expectations may have become even higher in the past decade as funding for other local organisations has declined sharply, reducing their capacity to deliver. However, hard pressed HEIs and their staff may start to see investment of time and resources in non-"core" (i.e. teaching and research) activities as an unjustifiable luxury in the face of shrinking budgets, wage restrictions and growing student demand.

Several Irish HEIs are located in or near to areas of high (or traditionally high) levels of deprivation. Many if not all HEIs encourage learners from non-traditional backgrounds through access programmes etc. As already outlined, IOTs are an important factor in engaging students from non-traditional backgrounds in HE. During the study visit for this review some concerns were expressed that the process of applying for designation as a technological university may cause a drift away from this strong local embeddedness as the merged institutions will operate across a much wider geography and will need to compete more at a national and international level for research funding.

Another way HEIs can contribute to society is by mobilising their staff and students through volunteering and community development activities (see Chapter 4). A commendable example is the NorDubCo initiative in North Dublin, which has established viable relationships with the business community, local government, the local development sector and education providers (Box 5.4).

Engagement in social and cultural development activities is an important way for HEIs to demonstrate their value and impact to their local communities. This can be an important element in building support for the value of higher education, particularly amongst communities that do not traditionally engage. Students can be a valuable resource to help with fundraising and providing support for services in the community. Formalising these opportunities (e.g. through course credits, formal recognition etc.) ensures a "win-win" for both sides and ensures supply matches demand. An example is the Child Law Clinic at University College of Cork (Box 5.5).

Internationalisation

Internationalisation constitutes a key strategic area for Irish HEIs. In the current expansion of study places, enrolments from Ireland and EU member countries are expected

> **Box 5.4. NorDubCo**
>
> NorDubCo was established in 1996 to promote social, economic and civic development of North Dublin. With the advent of the "Celtic Tiger" period of prolonged economic growth, many of the issues facing the region for which NorDubCo was established were no longer problematic. In others, economic growth had created a completely new set of issues to be addressed by the members of NorDubCo. Today's post-Celtic Tiger situation presents its own set of issues. Since its establishment NorDubCo has worked to ensure that sustainable economic, social and civic development takes place in the region. In this context it has worked to create a positive vision for community and working life in the region, a vision that sought to embrace all of the region's communities. NorDubCo's work had three distinct aims: to develop a more inclusive policy debate within the region; to promote new thinking to influence the economic, social and civic environment; and to enhance the effectiveness of NorDubCo. To this end, it involves the business community, local government, the local development sector, public representatives (both local and national), education (second-level, further), higher education, particularly with Dublin City University, and other local organisations, through projects such as the "Accelerated Skills Development Programme", and the "North Dublin Economic Clusters" project.
>
> *Source:* Source: NorDubCo (2017).

> **Box 5.5. Child Law Clinic at the University College of Cork**
>
> The Child Law Clinic at University College of Cork is a pro-bono legal research service provided by students for lawyers. Staffed by colleagues at the Faculty of Law, researchers and students on the Faculty's PhD and LLM programmes, the Clinic aims to enhance the quality of litigation in children's cases with a view to achieving progressive reform of child law in Ireland and internationally.
>
> The aims of the Child Law Clinic are to:
>
> 1. Improve the quality of children's representation
> 2. Promote evidence-based reform in all areas of child law
> 3. Support lawyers litigating children's issues
> 4. Provide students with practical experience of child law and litigation
>
> The Clinic does not provide legal advice to individuals but rather supports lawyers to represent and litigate on behalf of children. It also aims to provide legal support to organisations working with and for children.
>
> *Source:* UCC (2017).

to account for approximately two-thirds of the total increase with the rest coming from non-EU enrolments. In addition to internationalisation activities to boost outgoing and inward mobility of students and staff, it will be important to increase the number of opportunities and to build international links and relevant competencies for those students who will not go abroad during their studies.

Uptake of foreign language studies at second and third level is relatively low in Ireland compared to other European countries. For example, across the EU28 over 50% of upper secondary level students were studying two or more foreign languages, while in Ireland the figure was less than 10% (EUROSTAT, 2014). Ireland is also significantly below the EU28 average for adults speaking one or more foreign languages, with less than 30% compared to an EU28 average of over 60% (EUROSTAT, 2011). These factors constrain the ability of students to take part in exchange programmes and may also be a disincentive to some potential investors although employers often choose Ireland because they can attract international talent to locate here who have the native language skills required.

While the policy of recent years has been to emphasise the value of STEM subjects for the promotion of innovation and economic development, there should also be a similar "push" on studying foreign languages at second-level and third-level. In fact, courses in STEM fields could offer a language component, as it is often in these industries (especially technology) where the greatest demand for language skills originates. The Department for Education and Skills is currently working on a Foreign Languages in Education strategy.

At the University of Limerick (UL) a well-developed international alumni strategy includes a student ambassador programme and a scholarship initiative. UL has the largest outward mobility via the Erasmus programme of any Irish HEI.[4] It has the highest rating in Ireland in the international student barometer in terms of student experience, and is ranked fifth in the world. Significant resources are put into region-specific approaches to meet the need of partner institutions in terms of subject areas and qualification levels. For example, India is very interested in work placements and China in entrepreneurship. Courses are offered in French, German, Spanish, and Japanese. It is recognised that more could be done to keep links with incoming students after they return to their home institutions and international students in general. So far, only a few research activities have spun off from student mobility but there is potential for more. This is going to be acted upon by the newly established assistant deans, who will closely collaborate with the deans for academic affairs and research. It is also planned to introduce a "Challenge Fund for Internationalisation" for each faculty to seed fund innovative and promising initiatives. Faculties will set their own priorities and there will be a central co-ordinated assessment of how these contribute to UL's strategic plan.

Several promising initiatives have evolved also from the approach to internationalisation taken by the Limerick Institute of Technology (LIT). LIT currently has 200 international students which account for approximately 4% of the total student body. A recent focus has been on the "New Irish", who have a command of a number of languages which would be attractive to prospective employers and indeed other international partners who would welcome the opportunity to partner on exchange programmes with these students. LIT also places an emphasis on courses where students have a tendency to go abroad, instead of internationalising all programmes, as a way to build strong and lasting partnerships as opposed to creating a large number of short term partnerships.[5]

Dublin City University (DCU) also has a high number of international students (20% of total enrolments) from more than 100 countries. As in other HEIs, use is made of the national employment scheme for international students, which allows for up to 20 hours per week during term time, and 40 hours per week outside of term time for work in Ireland. There is also a "stay-back" scheme, whereby international students can remain for one year after graduating to work in Ireland.

Particularly on the part of SMEs, there seems to be some reluctance in taking foreign students on as the perception is that these students tend to leave shortly after the work placement ends. Information events which include the involvement of international students in collaborative research and other measures could help to raise awareness of opportunities which these students could gain and bring to (traditional) SMEs. The recently established Centre for Family Businesses at DCU is also expected to play a role in this. The Copenhagen Talent Bridge initiative (Box 5.6) offers relevant learning in this regard.

> **Box 5.6. Copenhagen Talent Bridge**
>
> Crucial for many economies and HEIs is the attraction and retention of internationally connected talents. This is also the aim of the Copenhagen Talent Bridge project which brings together all HEIs in Copenhagen, city governments and industry representatives in the Copenhagen area. One of the objectives is to support SMEs in hiring and managing international talents. There is both the demand for and supply of international skilled labour, but there are several barriers related to recruitment, language, daily work life, etc. which render employment difficult, especially for smaller firms. All HEIs located in Copenhagen have been important match-makers through their business links.
>
> The Copenhagen Talent Bridge project co-ordinates and scales these initiatives, functioning as a "talent pipeline" in key sectors such as cleantech, life sciences and ICT. Part of this is the Youth Goodwill Ambassador Corps, a global network of international students who, on a voluntary basis, represent Danish universities globally by sharing their personal experiences and organising events internationally.
>
> Source: HEInnovate (2017a).

Incentives can encourage universities and private institutions to collaborate for international funding competitions (e.g. Horizon 2020). This could include travel bursaries, buy-outs from other activities to develop proposals, training and capacity building, matchmaking services to help identify potential partners etc. Both the Science Foundation Ireland and Enterprise Ireland offer such support.

Building absorptive capacity

As well as these important supply side impacts, HEIs can also impact on the demand side of innovation through building absorptive capacity, supporting collaboration and providing local leadership for social and economic development initiatives. If Irish businesses do not have the capacity to absorb the research, knowledge and skills coming out of HEIs then the danger is that these "leak" out of the region or country to other places with higher innovation capacity, creating an "innovation paradox" (Ougthon et al., 2002) whereby high innovating places benefit from the investment made in lower innovating places, reinforcing the hierarchy of regions and countries as the strong places become ever stronger.

Building capacity in local companies creates not only potential value for the company in terms of innovation and growth opportunities but also helps build new potential partners for HEIs who may act as future collaborators, consultancy clients and employers for their graduates. According to latest available data, 99.8% of businesses in Ireland are SMEs, and 90.8% are micro SMEs, that is, they employ less than ten persons (Central Statistics Office, 2017). However SMEs only account for about two-thirds of employment in Ireland and less than half of gross value added (GVA). Therefore building capacity in this sector will be vital for sustainable future growth and development.

Many of the funding instruments designed to encourage collaborative activities between HEIs and business are geared towards businesses with ten or more employees, which are export oriented and operate in broadly STEM sectors. This effectively excludes over 90% of Irish businesses, which are arguably the ones that would benefit most from developing their capacity to absorb research and skills. The small proportion that does qualify is by definition innovative and growth oriented. There is a lack of evidence internationally (What Works Centre for Local Economic Growth, 2014) that supporting these businesses creates any significant additional benefits, that is, the attributed growth would probably have happened anyway.

Links with local businesses have often been made by academics carrying out short-term consultancy projects. In Ireland, controls on public sector pay and conditions may create restrictions on the wider institutional impact of these activities (see Chapter 3). Without links to individuals in the institution local businesses (especially the smaller ones) can find navigating the HEI to find the required support is a challenge.

Creating a more joined-up approach to businesses across the HEI through a single "front door", with clear offers for "transactional" services can help to build the relationships that lead to more transformational, long term engagements between businesses and HEIs. A corporate approach to client management can also help to ensure relationships do not "fall between the cracks", avoid duplication and ensure business get to the right part of the institution to meet their needs as quickly as possible. Student placements can act as a powerful tool in "breaking the ice" with businesses who have not previously engaged with HEIs and lead to longer term, more transformational relationships. They are also highly beneficial for students in terms of skills development and employability. A relevant example is the INaMi network in the Lüneburg region, which was initiated by Leuphana University (Box 5.7). Located between three large northern German agglomeration economies – Hamburg, Bremen and Hannover – the Lüneburg region is characterised by a high share of commuters and features of significant demographic change with areas of population increase as well as steep decrease. The regional labour market suffers from skills shortages and low firm-level innovation activity rates.

Box 5.7. INaMi network at Leuphana University

The INaMi network (*Innovationsverbund Nachhaltiger Mittelstand*) brings together SMEs from different sectors in an expert-moderated knowledge platform that provided access to research findings and generated practice-oriented knowledge. The network includes 74 SMEs from nine districts in the region and from more than 20 different sectors – e.g. food manufacturing, real estate, retailers, furniture manufacturing, architects, goldsmiths, stonecutters, elderly-care homes, mobility providers, industry laundry services, etc. The key issues these firms deal with on a daily basis are how to increase sales with sustainability-oriented products and services, and how to build management systems and an organisational culture that raises awareness and motivates employees.

Researchers from Leuphana University provided input knowledge in the form of short discussion papers for one-day conferences and regular working-group meetings (during the evenings and weekends), facilitated debates, and prepared documentary information, such as guidelines, checklists and handbooks. In total, INaMi organised 14 full-day events and 60 meetings for 17 working groups. 10 guidelines, 19 scientific publications and 60 news items were produced.

Through knowledge transfer and various capacity building activities, INaMi has fostered the absorptive capacity of local firms. Central to this have been twelve competence tandems,

> **Box 5.7. INaMi network at Leuphana University** *(cont.)*
>
> with teams of 10-30 scientists, each led by a Leuphana professor and an international scientist, as well as 19 R&D projects which involved around 600 firms through partnership agreements. In addition, scientists acted as expert facilitators in more than 80 thematic events, which applied highly innovative methods such as design thinking and involved more than 8 300 entrepreneurs, employees and local development actors.
>
> Through direct contacts with researchers and the development of background knowledge, these activities can be expected to have significantly raised the absorptive capacity of regional enterprises, and to have lowered the commonly present distance of small and traditional firms and other organisations in reverting to universities as providers of external knowledge for their innovation activities. Increasing numbers of joint applications for third-party funding, support services for regional firms, and collaborations with (high-)tech firms, who traditionally often seek collaborations with technical universities are indicators for this.
>
> *Source:* OECD, 2015.

Building collaborative capacity

HEIs, especially in institutionally "thin" places, are important actors in the social and economic development of the local area. Not only might they be the sole higher education provider (which is critical in a country like Ireland where student mobility is so low), but often they will be one of the largest employers and purchasers of goods and services in the area. Therefore it is essential that HEIs have a seat at the table with other public, private and social sector partners when designing development strategies, and where there is more than one HEI that they collaborate in order to design and deliver the appropriate programmes to meet local need and opportunity. Here, the Regional Clusters and the Regional Skills Fora play an important role.

HEIs are often seen as neutral brokers in local development who are able to "rise above" the (perceived) narrow financial or political concerns of the private and public sectors. There are a number of excellent examples of how HEIs are doing this in Ireland. However, HEIs cannot be expected to respond to every demand made on them by society without it resulting in a neglect of their "core" mission to deliver teaching and research. HEIs operate in a national and international as well as a local context. They cannot orient all of their teaching and research solely to the needs of the local economy.

Choices may have to be made which might not be popular with other partners. What should be the criteria for selecting what to do (and what *not* to do?) Furthermore other local actors might need to look to HEIs outside the locality for the expertise they need. What are the terms of engagement for HEIs that are less aligned to local needs? These are questions that influence strategic orientation and long-term development plans of HEIs and their engagement activities.

Effective local collaborations can result in mutually beneficial relationships with the overall impacts being greater than the sum of the individual parts. There may also be longer term benefits in terms of job and business opportunities as new products and services are developed as a result. Collaborative relationships for one purpose can create new opportunities for other activities. For example, a company that has worked on a skills development programme with an HEI might then use the relationship to start building a research collaboration.

Concepts such as societal challenges, social innovation, and quadruple helix are increasingly emerging as important for research aimed at addressing current and future major global challenges and their local implications. HEIs are often better placed than private or other traditional research organisations to work in these spaces as they house the cross-cutting and multidisciplinary knowledge and skills needed and are not (necessarily) working to tight deadlines as are those engaged in research aimed at more immediate commercial applications. An example is the NetwellCASALA research initiative at Dundalk Institute of Technology (Box 5.8).

> **Box 5.8. NetwellCASALA at Dundalk Institute of Technology**
>
> Population ageing is wrought with challenges, but it also offers many opportunities. At NetwellCASALA multidisciplinary research and development activities are focused on developing more integrated community-oriented services, more sustainable home and neighbourhood design, and more age-friendly technologies. Working closely with business partners, members of the community, health services, local and national government agencies, other academic establishments and ageing affiliated agencies, the project aims to translate ideas into practical solutions that improve the lives of older people and those who care for them, while also creating new business opportunities and informing public policies.
>
> NetwellCASALA is a joint venture between Dundalk Institute of Technology, the Health Service Executive of Ireland and Louth County Council. It has established links with a global network of stakeholders, placing it at the forefront of understanding of ageing and age-friendliness. Its activities involve an array of disciplines including the social and behavioural sciences, health and medical sciences, computer science, engineering, design, marketing and business administration.
>
> Working across the three inter-related and mutually reinforcing strands of communities, environment and technologies its researchers are able to provide partners with a complete concept-to-trial, product and service development environment through the NetwellCASALA Living Lab.
>
> *Source:* Interviews at Dundalk Institute of Technology during the study visit for this review in October 2015.

Conclusions

There are significant opportunities for HEIs to impact on their local economies, not only directly but in a wide range of indirect ways, both on the supply and demand side. However there is also a range of tensions that need to be understood and carefully managed by the HEIs themselves, their local partners and national policy makers if impacts are to be effectively delivered. From the analysis in this chapter of the tensions and challenges HEIs face in delivering impact and how these might be managed or overcome, it becomes clear that the higher education sector as a whole needs to make its case more powerfully by explaining to the public, as well as politicians and policy makers, the impact it is having in driving social and economic development and why this justifies significant investment. A national, sector-wide approach may be the best way forward rather than individual institutions each telling their own "story" in a different way.

Notes

1. These range from a factor 5 according to Zhang et al. (2015) to factor 7.5 according to Biggar Economics (2013).

2. Enterprise refers to entrepreneurial skills in the broader sense which are also important for developing skills in the future workforce to ensure they make the maximum contribution to productivity and growth in public, private and third sector organisations.

3. Defined as being over 23 years of age. In Irish higher education mature learners are students that are at least 23 years of age at the time they enter the study programme.

4. The Erasmus office maintains contacts with 280 Erasmus partners and 40 non-EU institutions.

5. These include study programmes in Fashion, Agriculture Mechanisation, Science, and various Level 8 programmes in Business Studies, Tourism, Events and Sports management.

References

BiGGAR Economics (2013), *Socio-Economic Impact Study of Dundalk Institute of Technology*, published online, www.campusengage.ie/sites/default/files/resources/Socio-Economic%20impact%20of%20DkIT%20final%20report%2019feb13.pdf (accessed 11 February 2017).

Central Statistics Office (2017), "Key statistics on small and medium-sized enterprises" website, www.cso.ie/en/releasesandpublications/ep/p-bii/businessinirelandabridged2012/smallandmediumenterprises/ (accessed 14 February 2017).

Department of Education and Skills (2015), *Country Background Report Ireland*, prepared for the HEInnovate Ireland country review, unpublished report submitted to the OECD.

Dorrity, C. (2010), "The third sector and the university: Reviewing needs and opportunities", *Critical Social Thinking: Policy and Practice*, 2, 117-129.

Dublin City University (2015), *Capturing the Economic and Social Value of Higher Education: A Pilot Study of Dublin City University*, published online, www.dcu.ie/sites/default/files/community/pdfs/Report2014.pdf (accessed 11 February 2017).

EPRSC (n.d.), *Welcome to the IDEAS Factory...home of innovation since 2004*, published online, www.epsrc.ac.uk/funding/howtoapply/routes/network/ideas/whatisasandpit/ (accessed 11 February 2017).

European Commission (2014), *Research and Innovation Performance and Horizon 2020 Country Participation for Ireland*, published online, http://ec.europa.eu/research/horizon2020/index_en.cfm?pg=country-profiles-detail&ctry=ireland, (accessed 14 February 2017).

EUROSTAT (2011), "Share of people aged 25–64 reporting they knew one or more foreign languages in 2011", published online, http://ec.europa.eu/eurostat/statistics-explained/index.php/File:Share_of_people_aged_25%E2%80%9364_reporting_they_knew_one_or_more_foreign_languages,_2011_(%C2%B9)_(%25)_edu15.png (accessed 14 February 2017).

EUROSTAT (2014), Proportion of students learning two or more languages in upper secondary education, 2008-2014, published online, http://ec.europa.eu/eurostat/statistics-explained/index.php/File:Proportion_of_students_learning_two_or_more_languages_in_upper_secondary_education_(general),_2009_and_2014_(%C2%B9)_(%25)_YB16-II.png (accessed 14 February 2017).

Goddard, J., M. Coombes, L. Kempton and P. Vallance (2014), "Universities as anchor institutions in cities in a turbulent funding environment: vulnerable institutions and vulnerable places in England", *Cambridge Journal of Regions, Economy and Society*, 7(2), 307-325.

Gunnigle, P. and D. McGuire (2001), "Why Ireland? A qualitative review of the factors influencing the location of US multinationals in Ireland with particular reference to the impact of labour issues", *Economic and Social Review* 32, 1, 43-68.

Higher Education Authority (2013), *How Equal? Access to Higher Education in Ireland*, published online, www.hea.ie/sites/default/files/how_equal_0.pdf (accessed 11 February 2017).

Higher Education Authority (2016a), *Investing in National Ambition: A Strategy for Funding Higher Education*, Report of the expert group on future funding for higher education, published online, www.education.ie/en/Publications/Policy-Reports/Investing-in-National-Ambition-A-Strategy-for-Funding-Higher-Education.pdf (accessed 11 February 2017).

Higher Education Authority (2016b), "Making an Impact Competition 2016" website, www.hea.ie/news/making-impact-competition-2016 (accessed 11 February 2017).

Henderson, C. (2001), *Shaping the Future: The Economic Impact of Public Universities*, National Association of State Universities and Land Grant Colleges, Washington, DC.

Irish Congress of Trade Unions Community Sector Committee (2012), *Changes in Employment and Services in the Voluntary and Community Sector in Ireland, 2008-2012*, published online, *www.ceeds.ie/files/resources/downsizingcommunitysector.pdf* (accessed 14 February 2017).

NorDubCo (2017), "Advancing social, economic and civic innovation in North Dublin", website, *www.nordubco.ie/* (accessed 14 February 2017).

OECD (2015), *Lessons Learned from the Luneburg Innovation Incubator*, published online, *www.oecd.org/cfe/leed/FINAL_OECD%20Luneburg_report.pdf* (accessed 11 February 2017).

Ougthon, C., M. Landabaso and K. Morgan (2002), "The regional innovation paradox: Innovation policy and industrial policy", *Journal of Technology Transfer*, 27, 97-110.

Science Foundation Ireland (2016), "Irish Host Research Bodies eligible for SFI funding" website, *www.sfi.ie/funding/sfi-eligible-research-bodies.html*, (accessed 14 February 2017).

The Irish Independent (17 February 2012), "PayPal forced to 'import' 500 workers and warns of language skills crisis", published online, *www.independent.ie/irish-news/paypal-forced-to-import-500-workers-and-warns-of-language-skills-crisis-26876581.html* (accessed 11 February 2017).

The Work Foundation (2010), *Anchoring Growth: the Role of 'Anchor Institutions' in the Regeneration of UK Cities*, The Work Foundation Alliance Limited, London.

University Alliance (2009), *Concentration and Diversity: Understanding the Relationship between Excellence, Concentration and Critical Mass in UK Research*, published online *www.unialliance.ac.uk/wp-content/uploads/2011/05/Publication_Research_Concentration_and_Diversity.pdf* (accessed 11 February 2017).

University College of Cork (2017), "Child law clinic at University College of Cork" website, *www.ucc.ie/en/childlawclinic/overview/* (accessed 11 February 2017).

University of Limerick (2016), "'By the People, for the People': Bringing public participation back to politics", Case study, published online, *www.ulresearchimpact.com/wp-content/uploads/2014/10/Case-4-politics.pdf* (accessed 11 February 2017).

Western Development Commission (2014), *Where will Future Population Growth Occur? Regional Population Projections 2016-2031*, published online, *www.wdc.ie/wp-content/uploads/Reional-Pop-Projections-WDC-Report-Dec-2014.pdf* (accessed 11 February 2017).

What Works Centre for Local Economic Growth (2014), *Evidence Review Business Advice*, published online, *www.whatworksgrowth.org/public/files/Policy_Reviews/14-05-16-Business-Advice-Review.pdf* (accessed 11 February 2017).

Zhang, Q., C. Larkin and B.M. Lucey (2015), "The economic impact of higher education institutions in Ireland", *Studies in Higher Education*, http://dx.doi.org/10.1080/03075079.2015.1111324.

ANNEX

HEInnovate framework and good practice statements

> **1. Leadership and governance**
>
> Strong leadership and good governance are crucial to developing an entrepreneurial and innovative culture within an HEI. Many HEIs include the words "enterprise" and "entrepreneurship" in their mission statements, but in an entrepreneurial institution this is more than a reference. This section highlights some of the important factors an HEI may consider in order to strengthen its entrepreneurial agenda.

1. Entrepreneurship is a major part of the HEI's strategy.

An HEI should see itself as an entrepreneurial organisation and environment, held together by a common vision, values and mission. The strategy of an HEI should reflect its entrepreneurial aspirations and agenda.

To score highly, an HEI could, for example:

- Have a mission statement and written strategy, setting out an entrepreneurial vision for the future of the institution
- Have a strategy which clearly emphasises the importance of entrepreneurship, culturally, socially and economically
- Articulate a clear implementation plan to achieve its strategy and vision with clear objectives and key performance indicators
- Provide examples of how the strategy and vision create opportunities across all aspects of the institution and its wider community

2. There is commitment at a high level to implementing the entrepreneurial agenda.

A deep commitment at senior management level of an HEI is needed to drive the implementation of the entrepreneurial agenda.

To score highly, an HEI could, for example:

- Communicate the strategy across the institution, and make sure that it is understood as a priority by staff, students and stakeholders
- Ensure that there is a dedicated person at a high level/senior management responsible for the implementation of the entrepreneurial vision and strategy
- Provide a strategic roadmap presented in a simple format that is widely communicated throughout the HEI
- Articulate how the entrepreneurial strategy is regularly reviewed and revised to keep it up-to-date and relevant

3. There is a model in place for co-ordinating and integrating entrepreneurial activities across the HEI.

An HEI needs an effective model for co-ordinating and integrating innovative activities across the institution. There are a variety of models which can be used, such as:

- A dedicated person at senior management level
- A dedicated unit close to senior management
- Co-ordination linked to a specific staff or faculty member
- Co-ordination by a centre for entrepreneurship/innovation

To score highly, an HEI could, for example:

- Build on existing relationships and activities
- Co-ordinate and integrate entrepreneurial activities across departments, faculties and other centres
- Co-ordinate activities with other stakeholders within the local entrepreneurship ecosystem

4. The HEI encourages and supports faculties and units to act entrepreneurially.

An HEI with open, flexible and devolved approaches finds it easier to undertake innovative activities and speed up decision-making. An HEI should provide an environment that encourages idea creation and the emergence of new activities and initiatives.

To score highly, an HEI could, for example:

- Allow faculties or units within the institution to take full responsibility and ownership of the development of new structures and centres
- Ensure ownership of and allocate responsibility for the development of new activities and initiatives that stimulate entrepreneurial capacity
- Support the faculties or units through a range of incentives and rewards linked to the demonstration of entrepreneurial and innovative outcomes

5. The HEI is a driving force for entrepreneurship and innovation in regional, social and community development.

An HEI can play several roles in its community and wider ecosystem. One of the key functions of an HEI is to support and drive regional, social and community development.

To score highly, an HEI could, for example:

- Be actively involved in the development and implementation of the local, regional and/or national innovation and entrepreneurship strategies
- Provide general access to the facilities of the institution to others in the wider community
- Support start-ups and/or established companies in the region to enhance innovation and growth
- Have a strong presence in its communities, for example, by supporting local cultural and artistic activities

---

2. Organisational capacity: Funding, people and incentives

The organisational capacity of an HEI drives its ability to deliver on its strategy. If an HEI is committed to carrying out entrepreneurial activities to support its strategic objectives, then key resources such as funding and investments, people, expertise and knowledge, and incentive systems need to be in place to sustain and grow its capacity for entrepreneurship.

---

1. Entrepreneurial objectives are supported by a wide range of sustainable funding and investment sources.

Becoming an entrepreneurial HEI is an incremental and long-term organisational development process that requires a sustainable and diverse financial basis and access to key resources and investments.

To score highly, an HEI could, for example:

- Ensure a close link between its long-term commitment to investing in entrepreneurial and innovative activities and its financial strategy
- Continuously engage with funders and investors to secure financial resources to deliver on its objectives
- Aim for a balanced and diversified range of funding and investment sources, including in-kind contributions
- Reinvest revenues generated from leveraging their own research, teaching and third mission activities (self-funding)

2. The HEI has the capacity and culture to build new relationships and synergies across the institution.

All internal stakeholders, staff and students, have a role in supporting an HEI's entrepreneurial agenda. Encouraging dialogue and synergies between the administration, academic faculties and staff, students and management helps break down traditional boundaries, foster new relationships and exploit internal knowledge and resources.

To score highly, an HEI could, for example:

- Promote shared facilities across faculties
- Establish structures for staff-student dialogue and decision making
- Create and support interdisciplinary structures
- Support cross-faculty teaching and research groups

3. The HEI is open to engaging and recruiting individuals with entrepreneurial attitudes, behaviour and experience.

An HEI can build an entrepreneurial culture and fulfil its objectives by engaging stakeholders with a strong entrepreneurial background and experience. These individuals can bring different viewpoints, knowledge, and expertise unavailable internally. Such individuals can be permanent members of staff, guest contributors, visiting associates or external stakeholders.

To score highly, an HEI could, for example:

- Demonstrate the importance it attaches to bringing in people with diverse backgrounds
- Give status and recognition to those who contribute to the institution's entrepreneurial agenda
- Recruit individuals with strong entrepreneurial backgrounds from the private, public or voluntary sectors and outside of academia
- Have mechanisms in place for shared risk and rewards in engaging in entrepreneurial opportunities

4. The HEI invests in staff development to support its entrepreneurial agenda.

Staff, both academic and administrative, are a key and necessary resource required to deliver on all elements of an HEI's entrepreneurial agenda, including the delivery of entrepreneurship education, provision of support for business start-ups, development of partnerships with other external stakeholders and supporting local and regional development.

To score highly, an HEI could, for example:

- Have a formal policy for career development for all staff linked to the implementation of the institution's entrepreneurial strategy and vision
- Set individual objectives and performance indicators for all staff supporting the implementation of the entrepreneurial agenda
- Measure staff progression against these objectives on a regular basis
- Link the training needs of staff with career objectives that support the entrepreneurial agenda

5. Incentives and rewards are given to staff who actively support the entrepreneurial agenda.

Encouraging and rewarding entrepreneurial behaviour in all staff reinforces the commitment to developing as an innovative HEI. This includes staff who actively seek out new opportunities to develop the institution in line with its strategic objectives. Incentive and reward systems should be available at an individual level as well as for faculties/departments, extending beyond classic career progression models.

To score highly, an HEI could, for example:

- Adjust staff teaching and research workloads for those who take on new responsibilities that support the institution's entrepreneurial agenda
- Provide institutional funds to staff to stimulate innovation and change
- Provide development sabbaticals for staff who seek to enhance their entrepreneurial capacity
- Instigate systems for rewards beyond traditional research, publications and teaching criteria
- Provide opportunities for professors to work part-time in their own companies (where permissible)
- Make office and laboratory space available for staff to pursue entrepreneurial activities

---

3. Entrepreneurial teaching and learning

Entrepreneurial teaching and learning involves exploring innovative teaching methods and finding ways to stimulate entrepreneurial mindsets. It is not just learning about entrepreneurship, it is also about being exposed to entrepreneurial experiences and acquiring the skills and competences for developing entrepreneurial mindsets.

---

1. The HEI provides diverse formal learning opportunities to develop entrepreneurial mindsets and skills.

An entrepreneurial HEI provides a range of learning opportunities to facilitate innovative teaching and learning across all faculties. Such an HEI should be encouraging innovation and diversity in its approach to teaching and learning across all departments as well as developing entrepreneurial mindsets and skills across all programmes.

To score highly, an HEI could, for example:

- Support curriculum change to stimulate and develop entrepreneurial mindsets and skills through new pedagogies, student-centred, cross-disciplinary and practice-based learning (e.g. living labs, the use of case studies, games and simulation)

- Provide support and training to staff in creating new curriculum related to entrepreneurship
- Provide mechanisms for students to engage in review and feedback on courses
- Introduce new mechanisms for supporting students, including experiencing starting new ventures within the students' formal education or delivering entrepreneurship education with practising entrepreneurs

2. The HEI provides diverse informal learning opportunities and experiences to stimulate the development of entrepreneurial mindsets and skills.

Extra-curricular learning opportunities are an important complementary part of entrepreneurship teaching and learning provision. An innovative HEI should offer a range of informal learning opportunities to students to inspire individuals to act entrepreneurially.

To score highly, an HEI could, for example:

- Support access to student enterprise clubs, awards and societies
- Organise networking events between students and entrepreneurs/businesses
- Engage students in business idea/plan competitions as part of their extra-curricular opportunities
- Formally recognise extra-curricular activities

3. The HEI validates entrepreneurial learning outcomes which drives the design and execution of the entrepreneurial curriculum.

An entrepreneurial learning experience provides opportunities to develop important skills and competences. These are essential for both graduate entrepreneurs as well as entrepreneurial graduates entering into employment. An HEI that values entrepreneurial learning commits to regular review, validation, and the updating of course content and learning outcomes across all study programmes.

To score highly, an HEI could, for example:

- Codify the expected entrepreneurial learning outcomes in relation to knowledge, skills and competences in all degree programmes
- Ensure students have a clear understanding of the entrepreneurial learning outcomes expected and achieved
- Validate entrepreneurial learning outcomes at the institutional level
- Recognise entrepreneurial learning outcomes in the students' records of achievements

4. The HEI co-designs and delivers the curriculum with external stakeholders.

External stakeholders are an important source of expertise that can be used in entrepreneurial teaching and learning. Regular engagement with external stakeholders encourages long-term collaborative relationships that can provide useful inputs to understanding future skills needs as well.

To score highly, an HEI could, for example:

- Regularly review and assess the involvement of external stakeholders in course design and delivery
- Provide a mechanism for staff to work with external stakeholders to develop and deliver high quality course content
- Integrate external stakeholders' experience and expertise into the development and delivery of extra-curricular learning activities and support services

- Support a diversity of collaborative partnerships with local communities and organisations, local and regional governments, chambers of commerce, industry and HEI alumni

5. Results of entrepreneurship research are integrated into the entrepreneurial education offer.

For a curriculum to stay up-to-date and relevant, the entrepreneurial education offer needs to be continuously reviewed and updated. Therefore an HEI should integrate the results of entrepreneurship research into its teaching.

To score highly, an HEI could, for example:

- Encourage staff and educators to review the latest research in entrepreneurship education
- Provide a forum whereby staff and educators can exchange new knowledge and ideas, incorporating the latest research
- Provide access to inspiration from other HEIs through networking and sharing good practices

---

4. Preparing and supporting entrepreneurs

HEIs can help students, graduates and staff consider starting a business as a career option. At the outset it is important to help individuals reflect on the commercial, social, environmental or lifestyle objectives related to their entrepreneurial aspirations and intentions. For those who decide to proceed to start a business, or other type of venture, targeted assistance can then be offered in generating, evaluating and acting upon the idea, building the skills necessary for successful entrepreneurship, and importantly finding relevant team members and getting access to appropriate finance and effective networks. In offering such support, an HEI should ideally act as part of a wider business support ecosystem rather than operating in isolation.

---

1. The HEI increases awareness of the value of entrepreneurship and stimulates the entrepreneurial intentions of students, graduates and staff to start up a business or venture.

Raising awareness of entrepreneurship in an HEI is about helping people make informed decisions about their careers, including the option of starting an enterprise.

To score highly, an HEI could, for example:

- Provide conducive framework conditions for start-up, such as enabling staff to own shares, work part-time, take sabbaticals, and the possibility for students to extend the duration of their study programmes to support starting a new venture while studying
- Make effective use of communication channels to raise awareness of opportunities and showcase entrepreneurship among staff and students across all parts of the institution
- Celebrate and recognise successes of student, graduate and staff entrepreneurs
- Provide opportunities for students to be involved in research projects leading to entrepreneurial opportunities and to take up internships with entrepreneurs

2. The HEI supports its students, graduates and staff to move from idea generation to business creation.

An HEI can support motivated students, graduates and staff in taking their first steps in preparing for a start-up. This includes developing an idea, finding a team, and exploring the technical and market feasibility of a project. As well as introducing staff to new networks, an HEI can offer regular activities to generate and evaluate business ideas emerging across the institution.

To score highly, an HEI could, for example:

- Offer entrepreneurial team building support and conflict management
- Provide intellectual property assistance for potential start-ups
- Create an expert advisory panel for early-stage concepts
- Organise interdisciplinary idea generation activities (e.g. start-up weekends)
- Organise idea and start-up pitch prizes
- Offer funds to support market feasibility studies

3. Training is offered to assist students, graduates and staff in starting, running and growing a business.

Entrepreneurship training can provide some of the skills and competences needed to start, run and grow a business. The training should impart relevant knowledge and skills about a wide range of topics, for example financing, legal and regulatory issues, dealing with people and building relationships, managing innovation processes, coping with success, stress and risk, and how to restructure or exit. Emotional preparation is as important as the technical aspects.

To score highly, an HEI could, for example:

- Offer tailored entrepreneurship courses across all subject areas and levels of study
- Actively recruit students and staff to training activities and monitor levels of engagement
- Involve entrepreneurs and key actors from the entrepreneurship ecosystem
- Use up to date teaching methods focused on learning-by-doing and critical reflection
- Implement mechanisms to increase rates of take-up by diverse groups

4. Mentoring and other forms of personal development are offered by experienced individuals from academia or industry.

Mentoring and other personal development relationships (such as coaching and tutoring) can help start-up entrepreneurs identify and overcome problems and develop their business networks. They provide valuable support in the form of knowledge, experience, social capital and encouragement on a long-term basis. Mentors and coaches tend to be experienced (academic) entrepreneurs, company managers and often alumni.

To score highly, an HEI could, for example:

- Organise visible, accessible and good-quality mentoring and personal development activities
- Actively recruit mentors and provide them with training, resources (e.g. IP assistance), formal recognition and rewards
- Facilitate matchmaking of mentors and protégés
- Provide feedback mechanisms on the contributions from entrepreneurs
- Provide opportunities for peer-to-peer mentoring, such as entrepreneur clubs, where members help each other

5. The HEI facilitates access to financing for its entrepreneurs.

External financing can be essential for the success of a new venture, e.g. providing investment for feasibility and market studies, product and prototype development such as proof of concept funding, for initial production or for offering the founders some living income before their first revenues are generated.

To score highly, an HEI could, for example:

- Offer financial education to entrepreneurs and potential entrepreneurs to better understand financial concepts and how to apply them
- Organise networking and financing events for aspiring entrepreneurs to pitch their ideas to investors and to get feedback
- Offer microfinance instruments such as grants, prizes, loans and equity
- Utilise its network of potential investors for crowd-funding
- Closely link access to financing activities with training, mentoring and incubation

6. The HEI offers or facilitates access to business incubation.

Business incubators commonly provide a range of services such as free or subsidised premises, access to laboratories and research facilities, prototyping support, IT and secretarial services and networking. They also offer a visible and accessible location for entrepreneurs to access an integrated package of coaching, mentoring, training, shared platforms and financing.

To score highly, an HEI could, for example:

- Host their own incubators or facilitate easy access to external incubators
- Ensure that their incubators offer a full range of soft support (networking, mentoring, etc.) as well as physical infrastructure
- Promote the incubator widely across campus and host events that engage potential entrepreneurs
- Embed the incubation facilities with the research and education infrastructure of the HEI to enhance synergies

---

5. Knowledge exchange and collaboration

Knowledge exchange is an important catalyst for organisational innovation, the advancement of teaching and research, and local development. It is a continuous process which includes the "third mission" of an HEI, defined as the stimulation and direct application and exploitation of knowledge for the benefit of the social, cultural and economic development of society. The motivation for increased collaboration and knowledge exchange is to create value for the HEI and society.

---

1. The HEI is committed to collaboration and knowledge exchange with industry, the public sector and society.

Knowledge exchange through collaboration and partnerships is an important component of any innovative HEI. It provides the opportunity to advance organisational innovation, teaching and research while creating value for society.

To score highly, an HEI could, for example:

- Ensure knowledge exchange and collaboration is a high priority at senior level and that implementation is in line with the institution's entrepreneurial agenda

- Establish structures to exploit knowledge exchange and collaboration opportunities, and encourage staff to engage in such activities
- Include support mechanisms for co-ordinating and sharing relationships across the HEI
- Give guidance on how to develop and implement all types of relationships with the public and private sector

2. The HEI demonstrates active involvement in partnerships and relationships with a wide range of stakeholders.

An innovative HEI understands the value of engaging with multiple stakeholders. There are many types of organisation with whom an HEI can form partnerships. These include, for example, regional and local organisations, quasi-public or private organisations, businesses (SMEs, large and international firms, social enterprises and entrepreneurs), schools and alumni.

To score highly, an HEI could for example:

- Involve external stakeholders in the work of the institution through governance, teaching, research, support for student activities and positions with institutes and centres
- Play an active role in influencing regional governance and regional/local development including entrepreneurship development
- Support entrepreneurship development of schools and colleges through networking and broader engagement
- Provide monitoring and feedback of the mutual value developed through stakeholder relationships

3. The HEI has strong links with incubators, science parks and other external initiatives.

Knowledge intensive structures surrounding an HEI provide opportunities to exchange knowledge and ideas. These include incubators, science parks and other initiatives. An innovative HEI should have systems in place that allow both inward and outward flows of knowledge and ideas.

To score highly, an HEI could, for example:

- Encourage the joint use of facilities
- Have direct financial or management interest in science parks and incubators, ranging from participation to ownership
- Ensure that the flow of people is incentivised in both directions
- Monitor the added value generated through linkages and cross-fertilisation activities

4. The HEI provides opportunities for staff and students to take part in innovative activities with business/the external environment.

An entrepreneurial HEI engages with the external environment through a variety of innovative activities. These can range from informal activities, such as breakfast clubs and networking events, through to more formalised initiatives including internships, learning factories, collaborative research and entrepreneurship projects.

To score highly, an HEI could, for example:

- Provide open spaces and facilities for collaboration with external actors
- Organise events that encourage engagement with external stakeholders, such as lectures, joint workshops, breakfast meetings and other networking events and opportunities

- Encourage, support and recognise mobility of staff and students through internships, sabbaticals, dedicated study programmes (e.g. industrial doctorates, sandwich programmes)

5. The HEI integrates research, education and industry (wider community) activities to exploit new knowledge.

Strong relationships with the external environment help stimulate the creation of new knowledge. An innovative HEI should integrate and assimilate the knowledge generated for extending its entrepreneurial agenda.

To score highly, an HEI could, for example:

- Have mechanisms in place to integrate and absorb information and experience from the wider ecosystem
- Monitor research activities regionally, nationally and internationally to identify new and relevant knowledge
- Initiate dialogue and discussion between the HEI and the external environment for mutual benefit
- Provide support for the identification of new ideas and their mutual exploitation
- Have clear mechanisms for exploiting entrepreneurial opportunities with commercial and industrial partners

---

6. The internationalised institution

Internationalisation is the process of integrating an international or global dimension into the design and delivery of education, research, and knowledge exchange. Internationalisation is not an end in itself, but a vehicle for change and improvement. It introduces alternative ways of thinking, questions traditional teaching methods, and opens up governance and management to external stakeholders. Therefore, it is linked very strongly to being entrepreneurial. It is not possible for an HEI to be entrepreneurial without being international, but the HEI can be international without being entrepreneurial or innovative.

---

1. Internationalisation is an integral part of the HEI's entrepreneurial agenda.

An international perspective is a key characteristic of an entrepreneurial and innovative HEI. Most institutions have internationalisation strategies and an innovative HEI will harmonise its internationalisation strategy and entrepreneurial agenda.

To score highly, an HEI could, for example:

- Ensure the internationalisation strategy reflects its entrepreneurial agenda
- Build common objectives and synergies between internationalisation and the entrepreneurial agenda

2. The HEI explicitly supports the international mobility of its staff and students.

International mobility brings in new educational and research ideas, creates intercultural opportunities and long lasting partnerships. In addition to attracting international staff and students, an entrepreneurial HEI actively encourages and supports the international mobility of its own staff and students.

To score highly, an HEI could, for example:

- Link international mobility objectives with the entrepreneurial agenda of the HEI

- Promote international mobility through exchange programmes, scholarships, fellowships and internships
- Apply for European mobility programmes and support the application of staff and students to mobility grants, scholarships and programmes
- Incentivise, recognise and reward international mobility

3. The HEI seeks and attracts international and entrepreneurial staff.

The internationalisation of an HEI depends upon people who can stimulate new approaches to teaching, learning and research in a global framework, using world-wide reputations and contacts to benefit the HEI's international network.

To score highly, an HEI could, for example:

- Explicitly set out to attract international staff which match the needs of its entrepreneurial agenda
- Have specific international recruitment drives in place
- Develop PhD programmes in collaboration with other partner institutions
- Have a support system in place for the cultural integration of international staff

4. International perspectives are reflected in the HEI's approach to teaching.

Access to new ideas for teaching and learning in the international environment can increase an HEI's ability to compete on the international market. Therefore an innovative HEI should have a teaching and learning environment tailored to a more global audience.

To score highly, an HEI could for example:

- Invest in an international-orientated curriculum which supports the institution's entrepreneurial agenda
- Ensure the curriculum is set up to prepare students for performing professionally and socially in an international and multicultural context
- Design and develop a curriculum which considers both "internationalisation abroad" and "internationalisation at home" experiences for staff and students
- Support international partnerships and networks which add value to teaching entrepreneurship
- Increase the number of joint/double degrees which include entrepreneurship and innovation in their curriculum
- Include classroom-based activities with an international perspective

5. The international dimension is reflected in the HEI's approach to research.

Strategic international research partnerships are an important part of an HEI's entrepreneurial agenda. The partnerships should be fully functional, not just paper agreements, and engage both staff and students.

To score highly, an HEI could, for example:

- Ensure that relationships with international research partners support its entrepreneurial agenda
- Develop extensive links with international research networks and innovation clusters
- Have internal support structures in place to manage and grow international relationships
- Use networks and partnerships to feed back into its research agenda
- Ensure all departments and faculties actively participate in international research partnerships and networks

> ### 7. Measuring impact
>
> Entrepreneurial/innovative HEIs need to understand the impact of the changes they bring about in their institution. The concept of an entrepreneurial/innovative HEI combines institutional self-perception, external reflection and an evidence-based approach. However, impact measurement in HEIs remains underdeveloped. The current measurements typically focus on the quantity of spin-offs, the volume and quality of intellectual property generation and research income generation, rather than graduate entrepreneurship, teaching and learning outcomes, retaining talent, the contribution to local economic development or the impact of the broader entrepreneurial agenda. This section identifies the areas where an institution might measure impact.

1. The HEI regularly assesses the impact of its entrepreneurial agenda.

The impact of the entrepreneurial agenda can be wide ranging across research, education and innovation, as well as within governance and leadership, depending on the type of HEI. Understanding whether objectives are being met is crucial, if an HEI is to achieve its intended outcomes.

To score highly, an HEI could, for example:

- Set clear intended outcomes/impacts related to its entrepreneurial agenda
- Collect evidence of the outcomes/impacts of the entrepreneurial agenda
- Use the evidence of the outcomes/impacts as a tool for reflection and review of the strategy and mission of the institution

2. The HEI regularly assesses how its personnel and resources support its entrepreneurial agenda.

Becoming an entrepreneurial institution may require an HEI to re-think how its personnel and resources are employed. An HEI may need to develop new human resource strategies, leverage external partnerships to overcome internal shortcomings, and secure new sources of financial support.

To score highly, an HEI could, for example:

- Undertake a skills/competence audit against the entrepreneurial agenda to assess its institutional development needs
- Use the information from the skills assessment and embed in recruitment strategies and staff performance appraisals
- Leverage external partners and resources to address any skills gaps
- Review and assess the success of the allocation of personnel and resources at regular intervals

3. The HEI regularly assesses entrepreneurial teaching and learning across the institution.

Ensuring that entrepreneurial teaching activities reach their full potential requires systematic assessment across all faculties and departments. An entrepreneurial HEI should have set clear objectives, which are regularly monitored and evaluated, and the results fed back into course renewal and staff development plans.

To score highly, an HEI could, for example:

- Set clear objectives for the impact of entrepreneurship courses and activities

- Measure the impact of entrepreneurship teaching and learning at different phases of its implementation (beginning, end, point in time after) to get an accurate picture of change
- Measure changes in participants' motivation and the level of knowledge, skills and competences gained through the entrepreneurship education activities
- Track findings over time and across all faculties and departments

4. The HEI regularly assesses the impact of start-up support.

It is important to monitor and evaluate start-up support activities to ensure that they are providing the appropriate quality of support in an effective manner. An entrepreneurial HEI should also examine outreach, take-up and the role played by start-up support across all faculties and departments.

To score highly, an HEI could, for example:

- Set clear objectives and intended outcomes/impacts for start-up support activities, including participation rates, satisfaction and outcomes
- Measure the intended outcomes/impacts immediately following the end of support measures and at later dates to measure the success in relation to start-ups
- Ensure the findings are fed back into the development of start-up support activities

5. The HEI regularly assesses knowledge exchange and collaboration.

Assessing and gaining a better understanding of the HEI's knowledge exchange and collaborative activities can result in increased value creation for both the institution and society. Therefore, an innovative HEI should have mechanisms and activities in place to regularly monitor and evaluate the intended outcomes and impacts of these activities across all faculties and departments.

To score highly, an HEI could, for example:

- Set clear objectives and intended outcomes/impacts for knowledge exchange linked to its entrepreneurial agenda
- Set internal measurements of success such as new research ideas generated, joint HEI-business projects and relationships formed, number of start-ups and spins-offs created
- Set external measurements of success, such as perceived value and impact of the HEI on the wider environment (e.g. business, government)
- Assess these intended outcomes/impacts from an internal and external viewpoint
- Use the evidence of success as a tool for reflection and review of the entrepreneurial agenda

6. The HEI regularly assesses the institution's international activities in relation to its entrepreneurial agenda.

Having an international perspective is a key characteristic of an entrepreneurial HEI. An entrepreneurial HEI should regularly monitor and evaluate whether its internationalisation strategy supports the development of its entrepreneurial agenda across all faculties and departments.

To score highly, an HEI could, for example:

- Set clear objectives and intended outcomes/impacts for internationalisation activities linked to its entrepreneurial agenda
- Undertake regular mapping exercises of the internationalisation activities in teaching and research to prioritise and further develop its entrepreneurial activities
- Use the evidence of success as a tool for reflection and review of its internationalisation and entrepreneurial agenda.

OECD PUBLISHING, 2, rue André-Pascal, 75775 PARIS CEDEX 16
(87 2017 01 1 P) ISBN 978-92-64-27088-6 – 2017

Lightning Source UK Ltd.
Milton Keynes UK
UKHW050631100320
360091UK00004B/254